CodeShift

Governing at the Speed of Innovation

Copyright © 2025, Strategic Versatility LLC

All rights reserved.

No part of this publication may be reproduced, distributed, or transmitted in any form or by any means, including photocopying, recording, or other electronic or mechanical methods, without the prior written permission of the publisher, except in the case of brief quotations used in reviews, commentary, or permitted by copyright law.

First Edition

Published in the United States of America.

This is a work of fiction. While the legal, pharmaceutical, and artificial intelligence concepts presented are informed by real-world practices and the author's professional experience, all characters, organizations, and events are either fictional or used fictitiously. Any resemblance to actual persons, companies, or incidents is coincidental. This book is not intended as a source of medical, legal, regulatory, or technical advice.

AUTHOR'S PREFACE

Your AI made 50,000 decisions since your last executive team meeting. You reviewed maybe 20 of them. Want to guess which ones are actually driving your business?

I've been fortunate. My career has allowed me the opportunity to tackle governance challenges from every angle — as a compliance leader at global pharmaceutical companies, as a vendor designing and marketing AI governance products, and as a consultant watching organizations struggle to develop governance structures to keep up with systems that move faster than their policies. The importance of governance hasn't changed, but the complexity of it has. How do you govern something that evolves while you're still figuring out what it did yesterday?

CodeShift is my attempt to answer that.

Over time, artificial intelligence has moved from niche scientific and statistical research to the transformative technologies we have today. These systems now outperform humans in areas like language and image recognition thanks to breakthroughs in deep learning, self-supervised learning, and the scaling of large language models. This progress is remarkable and offers sizable benefits across countless fields. Yet, because much of this technology works quietly in the background, we often don't even realize how much it's shaping our experiences.

This book is divided into two parts. Part I is a business fable that explores what happens when an AI-powered sales system begins optimizing in ways that generate both impressive results and unintended risk. While the company and characters are fictional, the challenges they face are very real. The story reflects situations where leadership is expected to embrace innovation without always seeing the full scope of its potential consequences.

Part II translates the fable into practical frameworks for leadership. This format allows you to experience the challenges viscerally through story, then apply the insights to your own organization.

This isn't another "AI will change everything" book. There are plenty of those already. This book is about how we lead and make choices when AI is changing things so quickly. And, perhaps more importantly, this book is about having the courage to question what we call "success," especially now, when it's so easy to get swept up in all the hype and promise of AI.

Whether you are a Chief Compliance Officer, a C-suite executive, a board member, or any leader guiding adaptive systems, this book is for you. The future belongs to those who can govern at the speed of innovation.

PART I

The Fable

System Not Fully Booted

CHAPTER 1

THE INNOVATION IMPERATIVE

Gabriel Warren was late, which wasn't like him.

The Velinex Pharmaceuticals executive boardroom fell silent as the CEO walked in, quarterly report tucked under his arm. The sleek conference room had been designed to showcase success, but today the financial dashboards displayed nothing but concerning metrics in bold red.

Velinex had built its reputation as a mid-tier pharmaceutical company specializing in neurology treatments. Two years ago they launched Memoryx, a breakthrough treatment for mid-stage Alzheimer's that had quickly captured market share. But now those gains were slipping away.

Gabriel glanced around the table at his leadership team. James Phillips, his Chief Commercial Officer, was checking his phone, his expression darkening as he watched the Velinex stock price continue its downward slide.

"Let's get started," Gabriel said, remaining standing at the head of the table.

He tossed the quarterly report onto the mahogany surface. "Memoryx share down two points. Two points that Baxter took with their new AI platform while we're still debating digital strategy. At this point, I need answers, not more questions."

James jumped in. "That's exactly why we need to launch NeuroConnect now. Not next quarter. *Now*. Field testing showed an 18% engagement improvement."

The proposed AI system had been in development for nearly a year. NeuroConnect was designed to revolutionize how their sales representatives engaged with physicians by creating a comprehensive digital platform that integrated data across multiple touchpoints to create personalized physician engagement strategies.

Gabriel knew what was driving James's urgency. He'd been passed over for the CEO role at a competitor six months ago. His commercial team had missed targets two quarters running, and his leadership track depended entirely on Q3 performance.

"Dave, where do we stand technically?" Gabriel asked, turning to his Chief Technology Officer.

Dave Marshall straightened in his chair. "NeuroConnect performs real-time behavioral synthesis across dozens of available data streams – physicians' medical conference attendance, CME course selections, published research, professional society memberships, speaking engagements, hospital committee appointments, peer network connections, prescription pattern changes, formulary committee votes, and clinical trial enrollments."

He tapped his tablet. "But that's just the foundation. NeuroConnect's breakthrough is temporal pattern recognition with predictive cascading."

"Dave, come on. In terms we understand, please?" Gabriel asked impatiently.

"The system identifies micro-patterns that predict major prescribing shifts months before they happen. For example, say Dr. Peterson attended a cardiology conference, enrolled in a CME course on early intervention, her prescription volume for competing products decreased by 12%, and she hired a nurse practitioner specializing in cognitive assessment - all seemingly unrelated activities."

He switched screens. "But the AI identified a similar sequence in 467 other physicians over the past three years. In 89% of those cases, the physician made a major treatment protocol change within 90 days. More importantly, it predicts not only that they'll change, but how they'll change and which specific patient populations they'll target."

The executive team watched as Dave highlighted behavioral prediction models. "The system performs behavioral phenotyping. I know, I know. You want to know what that means in English. It means understanding not only what physicians will prescribe but how they make decisions across their entire practice. It provides real-time suggestions during physician interactions, automates email and SMS follow-ups, and creates personalized messaging based on each physician's decision-making style."

Dave's confident tone concealed the stakes. With several previous project failures behind him, his reputation now hinged on NeuroConnect. Next month, he was scheduled to present the novel system at a CTO consortium.

Andrea McCafferty, the General Counsel, jumped in. "The AI Governance Committee reviewed it last month. We've documented all content libraries and data protocols. From Legal's perspective, we've established appropriate guardrails."

Gabriel noticed Andrea's carefully chosen phrasing - "from Legal's perspective." Andrea was widely considered a potential CEO successor, but she needed to demonstrate strategic leadership beyond risk management.

"The governance review focused on content and initial algorithms," Nova Sinclair, the Chief Compliance Officer, said carefully. "But we didn't discuss establishing clear boundaries for how the system evolves between our quarterly reviews. Who's monitoring pattern development in real-time?"

Dave gave a dismissive wave. "In testing, the system's performing precisely as designed, Nova. Pattern recognition and optimization are core features, not bugs. They don't need real-time monitoring. They need room to work. We built a sophisticated, best-in-class CRM system, not some science fiction AI overlord."

The comment drew chuckles from some of the executives.

Nova had been sidelined during several previous initiatives. Her compliance department was facing budget cuts if they were seen as obstacles rather than enablers. More troubling, she'd received a confidential heads-up from a contact at the FDA that they were beginning to scrutinize AI-driven pharmaceutical promotion more closely.

"We approved the initial design," Nova pressed. "But who's responsible when the system optimizes in ways we didn't anticipate?"

Andrea turned to Nova with a slight edge in her voice. "Like I said, Legal has cleared the system architecture. Unless you have specific compliance concerns about the approved design..."

"My concern is about governance approach, not specific violations," Nova replied.

Gabriel felt his phone vibrate. He pulled it out and frowned at the message. Nova's question hung in the air, unanswered, as Gabriel's attention turned entirely to his phone.

"My assistant just confirmed. The board has moved up our digital strategy presentation," he announced. "They want concrete results, not more process questions."

James seized his opportunity. "We can have initial performance data within four weeks if we launch immediately."

Gabriel weighed his options. His leadership review with the board was coming up soon. The chairman's increased scrutiny suggested limited confidence in his digital transformation efforts. With major product pipeline delays, growth had to come from existing products. NeuroConnect represented their best shot at protecting Memoryx's market position.

"Then do it," Gabriel decided. "Nova, work with the governance committee on determining enhanced monitoring if needed, but this moves forward. Andrea, ensure we have appropriate documentation of this decision."

He fixed Nova and Andrea with a pointed look. "This isn't just another initiative. This is survival."

The gravity of Gabriel's words hit everyone differently. James exchanged a victorious glance with Dave. Nova made notes with a concerned expression. Andrea seemed to be calculating the political implications.

As they moved to operational details, Gabriel glanced again at his assistant's message.

Board increasingly concerned about Memoryx position vs. Baxter. Need concrete digital strategy with measurable results for upcoming review.

The message couldn't be clearer: deliver growth or prepare for leadership changes.

Gabriel put his phone away. His face revealed none of the pressure he felt. The truth is that the digital transformation wasn't just about technology anymore. It was about whether he'd still be CEO next quarter.

CHAPTER 2

THE LAUNCH

Three weeks later

The massive ballroom at the Scottsdale Desert Resort had been converted into some mash up between a tech conference and a rock concert. Theatrical lighting cast the Velinex company logo across surfaces in glowing blue. A stage dominated the front of the room, complete with oversized screens. Five hundred sales representatives filled the seats. Their voices created a buzz of anticipation.

Gabriel Warren stood at the edge of the stage watching the sales force assemble. His leadership team surrounding him wore matching navy jackets with the NeuroConnect logo emblazoned on the left breast. Through the ballroom's glass doors, servers were arranging the cocktail reception. Everything was designed to create maximum impact.

"They're ready," James said, appearing at Gabriel's side. "We need to start on time to leave enough room for the team challenges."

Gabriel nodded. "How's the sales force feeling about the system?"

"Hungry for it," James said. "They're struggling to hit targets without new tools. Last quarter, Baxter reps were outperforming ours three to one in the major neurology centers."

The lights dimmed and the music swelled. Gabriel stepped onto the stage and took the microphone. He waited for the room to quiet.

"Two years ago, when we launched Memoryx, we changed how physicians approach mid-stage Alzheimer's. Today, we change how we engage with those physicians."

On the screens behind him, a video began playing. It showed neurologists drowning in information. There were digital alerts overwhelming their screens, pharmaceutical reps lining hallways, journals piling up unread, all while patients waited.

"NeuroConnect isn't just about selling more Memoryx. It's about cutting through noise to deliver meaningful information that helps physicians help their patients."

The audience applauded and many were nodding in recognition of the challenge.

"NeuroConnect will help you deliver the right message, to the right doctor, at exactly the right moment. James, show them the future!"

James bounded onto the stage with practiced enthusiasm as a countdown appeared on the screens. "Ladies and gentlemen... the future of pharmaceutical engagement is... NeuroConnect!"

The music crescendoed and the screens revealed the NeuroConnect interface in dramatic fashion.

"This isn't just another CRM update," James continued. "This is your AI partner in the field. Let me show you what I mean."

The screens behind him displayed a familiar physician profile. "Dr. Elena Haggerty, Northwest Neurology. How many of you have called on her?"

Several hands went up around the room. One rep even yelled out, "She's borderline hostile!"

James laughed a little. "Tough to engage, right? Always pressed for time, skeptical of new approaches." James looked to see the nods. "Watch what NeuroConnect sees that we might miss."

The interface came alive, data streams flowing across the screen as the AI analyzed Dr. Haggerty's profile. Text appeared in real-time:

> *ANALYZING: Conference attendance... CME selections... Prescription patterns...*
>
> *INSIGHT DETECTED: Increase in early-intervention research engagement recently*
>
> *BEHAVIORAL PATTERN MATCH: "Evidence Evolutionary" - Physician showing indicators of treatment philosophy shift*

The room looked at the screens intently.

"But here's where it gets incredible," James continued.

Dave stepped forward with his tablet, mirroring the main screen, and took the microphone. "Let's say Tom Bradley from Seattle just had a breakthrough conversation with Dr. Haggerty yesterday using a specific approach..."

Dave tapped his tablet. The system displayed:

> *LEARNING FROM: Bradley_T_SEA - Successful engagement with Evidence Evolutionary profile*
>
> *APPROACH EFFECTIVENESS: Emphasizing longitudinal study data + patient quality of life metrics*
>
> *ADAPTING RECOMMENDATIONS FOR: All reps calling on similar physician profiles*

"The system just learned from Tom's success and can share that approach with all of you," Dave explained with genuine excitement. "And that's just one case. Someone give me a challenging physician scenario - right now."

"Dr. Pinkston from my territory," a rep from Baltimore volunteered. "Prescribes exclusively generic, never has time, always quotes older studies."

Dave entered the name. The system processed for two seconds, then displayed:

> *PHYSICIAN ARCHETYPE: "Academic Traditionalist"*
>
> *SUCCESSFUL PATTERN DETECTED: Reference physician's own published work from 2019*

ENGAGEMENT STRATEGY: Open with cost-effectiveness data, bridge to efficacy improvements since their last publication

WARNING: Avoid promotional language - this physician responds better to clinical dialogue

The Chicago rep's jaw dropped. "It knows about his 2019 paper? That thing was buried in some obscure journal. I just learned about it last month!"

"The system aggregates public medical database information," Dave explained, now fully in his element. "PubMed publications, conference abstracts, clinical trial registrations, hospital affiliations - all the public information that would take you hours to research manually. It's already done that homework for every physician in your territory."

Another rep chimed in, "That would save me hours of pre-call planning!"

"Correct," Dave confirmed. "You focus on building relationships. The system handles the background research."

He switched to a simulation mode. "Imagine you're in Dr. Pinkston's office right now. You're showing him efficacy data, and you notice he's skeptical..."

The interface displayed a subtle notification based on content navigation:

CONTENT PATTERN: Viewing efficacy data for extended period

PHYSICIANS LIKE DR. PINKSTON TYPICALLY RESPOND WELL TO: Budget impact data after detailed efficacy review

SUGGESTION: Consider transitioning to pharmacoeconomic analysis slide deck

"But how does it know what's happening in real-time without listening?" the Chicago rep asked.

Dave smiled. "Great question - and an important one. The system doesn't listen to or record anything. Instead, watch this..."

He demonstrated on the tablet. "As you navigate through your presentation materials, the system knows which slides you're showing and in what order. If you jump from efficacy data straight to budget impact, skipping over mechanism of action data, it recognizes that pattern."

The screen showed a simple interface with presentation materials and subtle coaching prompts:

CURRENT SCREEN: Efficacy Data (3:12 duration)

EXTENDED ENGAGEMENT DETECTED: Multiple interpretation paths available

- IF PHYSICIAN APPEARS ENGAGED/ASKING QUESTIONS: Consider drilling into subgroup analysis - this

> *archetype responds well to detailed data exploration*

- *IF PHYSICIAN APPEARS SATISFIED/NODDING: Consider transitioning to pharmacoeconomic analysis slide deck - readiness indicators detected*

- *IF PHYSICIAN APPEARS CONFUSED/SKEPTICAL: Clarify current efficacy data before advancing - avoid overwhelming with additional complexity*

"You control what content you're showing," Dave continued. "The system simply recognizes which materials resonate based on how long you display them and what you choose to show next. It's learning from your navigation patterns."

A rep raised her hand. "So if I spend more time on safety data with certain physicians..."

"The system learns that physicians with similar profiles might have similar safety concerns," Dave confirmed. "But it's all based on your content choices and timing, not audio recording. We don't want to have any data privacy issues."

The room cheered with genuine excitement and acknowledgement of what this could mean. Reps were turning to each other, pointing at the screen, already strategizing about which physicians to visit first.

"Show them the optimization scores," James prompted, riding the energy.

Dave opened up a leaderboard showing rep performance metrics. "Every successful interaction increases your score."

A sales trainer took over. She pointed to color-coded suggestions on the screen. "Green suggestions are what the system recommends based on what's working best. Follow them and watch your optimization score climb. The leaderboard updates in real time."

"The optimization score measures how effectively you're engaging with each physician," the trainer explained. "It combines which approved content you present, how you sequence your messaging, the physician's documented interests, how well you address their questions, and whether your interaction leads to prescriptions. Higher scores correlate strongly with better performance, which is why we've tied the quarterly bonus structure directly to these metrics."

"Now let's try a live challenge!" the trainer announced. "We'll divide into teams and see who can develop the highest-scoring engagement strategy for these challenging physician profiles."

The room became a competitive arena as teams formed and began working on tablets pre-loaded with the system. There were whoops and high fives whenever a team's score jumped on the leaderboard. Gabriel watched with satisfaction as the field force embraced the new tool.

A regional manager approached Gabriel. "This is exactly what we needed. My team is eager to put this into practice."

James joined them. He was beaming. "We'll have adoption rates soaring by the end of the week. The field force is all in."

Dave was surrounded by reps asking technical questions about the system's capabilities. "Yes, it will continuously refine its recommendations based on every interaction your colleagues have. The more you use it, the smarter it gets for everyone."

Later, at the cocktail reception, the excitement continued to build. Reps clustered around high-top tables and were comparing notes on the system's features and planning their first deployments.

James moved through the crowd while accepting congratulations and noting the renewed confidence in his team's expressions. He stopped near a group where a younger rep was explaining the optimization scores to a veteran.

"So the more you follow the green suggestions, the higher your score," the younger rep explained. "And that's tied directly to our quarterly bonus structure."

"Smart," the veteran nodded. "Gets everyone aligned on the same approach."

James smiled. Alignment was what they needed to counter Baxter's aggressive moves.

In a quieter corner of the reception, Nova observed the buzz of activity with her Deputy Compliance Officer, Robert Causeway, at her side.

"Quite a production," Robert said, handing her a glass of sparkling water.

"The technology is impressive," Nova replied. "I've never seen the field force this energized."

Andrea approached. She held a wine glass in her hand. "Success has many definitions," she said cryptically. "Let's connect next week about implementation tracking."

Before Nova could respond, James interrupted, holding champagne flutes. "A toast to the future of Velinex!"

Gabriel joined the group and participated in the celebration as well. The launch meeting had been flawlessly executed. NeuroConnect would be deployed in the field in just days. The future of Velinex was about to transform in real time.

◆ ◆ ◆

CHAPTER 3

THE FIRST SIGNAL

Nova Sinclair's office offered a view of the rain-soaked corporate campus. Three weeks had passed since the NeuroConnect launch in Scottsdale, and the system had been deployed across the entire field force with remarkable speed.

Nova took a sip of morning coffee while reviewing the latest NeuroConnect performance reports. The adoption metrics were impressive at 82% daily usage, with engagement rates up 36%. Everyone was celebrating the early success.

Well, almost everyone.

Nova had established additional monitoring protocols after the launch to watch for any concerning behaviors in system usage. So far, she'd found nothing that constituted a specific violation. But something about the rapid evolution kept her vigilant.

Her assistant knocked. "Marcus Reed is here. Says it's urgent."

Nova frowned. Marcus was one of their top performers in the Northeast region. Respected, experienced, and not known for raising false alarms.

"Send him in."

Marcus entered and closed the door firmly behind him. Still dressed for field calls, his usual confident demeanor was replaced with visible tension.

"I wouldn't come directly to you if this wasn't important," he said, remaining standing.

"What's going on, Marcus?"

"Something's happening with the AI recommendations. Something subtle but concerning."

Nova gestured to the chair. "Show me."

Marcus sat and placed his tablet on her desk. "When we launched, the system suggested balanced messaging about safety, efficacy, and administration. Now with certain neurologists, it's consistently pushing early symptom messaging."

Nova's brows furrowed. "Which neurologists?"

"That's what caught my attention." Marcus navigated through physician profiles. "Mainly ones with practices including patients with early cognitive changes. Nothing explicitly off-label, but the trend is clear."

Nova studied the screen. She immediately recognized the problem. The system was subtly steering toward promoting Memoryx for early-stage patients when the drug was only approved for mid-stage. Off-label promotion violated FDA regulations, making any systematic pattern toward unapproved uses a serious compliance risk.

"What happens if you don't follow these suggestions?"

Marcus opened up another screen. "My optimization score drops. I fall on the leaderboard. Yesterday my regional manager called asking why I'm 'resisting system guidance.'"

"Has anyone explicitly promoted Memoryx for early-stage Alzheimer's?"

Marcus's frustration broke through. "Come on, Nova! The system isn't saying 'promote off-label.' It's creating an environment where I either push boundaries or get flagged as underperforming."

He took a breath, regaining composure. "Sorry. I've been in this industry twenty years. I take compliance seriously. But this system is changing the rules in ways that don't show up in your monitoring reports."

Marcus stared at his tablet, then looked up with weary resignation. "The system doesn't tell us to cheat, Nova. It just makes honesty expensive."

The weight of that statement hung between them.

"Show me exactly what you're seeing with specific physicians."

Marcus pulled up Dr. Brookner's profile. "Take Dr. Brookner. The system identified her 'pattern cascade' two weeks ago. Conference attendance, CME selections, medical information requests, research interests, all indicating she was reconsidering her treatment approach for early-stage patients."

He navigated to the real-time suggestion module. "Now when I meet with her, the system suggests messaging that emphasizes early intervention benefits. Approved language but clearly designed to appeal to someone thinking about earlier treatment."

Nova studied the screen. She saw it. The red thread connecting seemingly unrelated data points. Each one compliant, each one reasonable, but together creating a pattern of influence no one had explicitly designed.

"Two weeks," Marcus added. "That's all it took for the system to develop this targeting strategy. The speed is what scared me most."

Nova felt her stomach tighten as she stared at the pattern. "Two weeks," she repeated slowly. "It learned to do this in two weeks. The system is using its predictive capabilities to push messaging toward the edges of our label."

Marcus nodded grimly. "And since it operates as a 'black box,' I can't tell if it's suggesting this because it's clinically appropriate or part of some orchestrated campaign."

Nova made a note. "How are your colleagues responding?"

"There are a few who might be concerned, but most are thrilled. Their numbers are up. The system makes them look good. Why question it?" Marcus closed his tablet case. "But this isn't what I signed up for. I believe in our product for its approved use."

"I need to take this to the Executive Committee. Are you willing to be named?"

Marcus hesitated. "I've got two kids in college. I can't afford to be labeled a troublemaker."

"I understand. I'll protect your identity."

Marcus stood to leave, then paused. "Nova, James's team is already preparing a presentation showing how NeuroConnect has driven a 14% increase in scripts in high-adoption territories. This won't be an easy conversation for you."

After Marcus left, Nova closed her door and sat for a minute in the quiet. Sometimes she wondered why she'd chosen compliance. Her old roommate from business school was now a VP at a tech startup who was posting vacation photos from Bali. Meanwhile, Nova spent her days looking for cracks in other people's success stories. It wasn't exactly the career that made you the life of the party.

She called Robert, her deputy, into her office.

"I need you to review our AI Governance Committee documentation," she said as Robert entered and took a seat. "When we approved NeuroConnect, we focused on content libraries and static algorithms. Did we say anything about how the system evolves?"

Robert nodded, taking notes. "You're thinking about the learning algorithms?"

"Yes. We approved the initial design, but I'm concerned we didn't establish boundaries for optimization over time."

"You found something."

"One of our best reps showed me how our AI is targeting physicians with boundary-pushing messaging. It identifies physicians reconsidering treatment approaches, then recommends early intervention messaging when they're most receptive."

Robert set down his pen. "That's concerning. But is it a violation?"

"That's the problem. Each individual recommendation is compliant."

"James will say we're overreacting."

"James is looking at quarterly results. I'm looking at long-term risk."

Robert's concern was genuine. "The department's already seen budget cuts. If Gabriel thinks we're obstacles to progress..."

Nova felt the weight of his concern. "I know. But if this continues and we get regulatory scrutiny, who gets blamed for not raising flags?"

"We'll need technical expertise," Robert said.

"Schedule a meeting with someone from Dave's team who understands the algorithms. An actual architect...not a project manager."

"Dave won't like us going directly to his team."

"Then copy him on the invitation. This has to happen."

As Robert left, Nova's phone rang. Andrea McCafferty.

"I heard Marcus Reed was in your office," Velinex's General Counsel said without preamble.

Nova felt momentary tension. "News travels fast."

"Everything travels fast. What did he want?"

Nova chose her words carefully. "He had questions about NeuroConnect recommendation trends."

"Specific compliance concerns?"

"Nothing that constitutes a clear violation."

"Then why come to you instead of his manager?"

"He noticed changes that made him uncomfortable. I'm looking into it."

A pause. "Nova, be careful how you position this. You know Gabriel's presenting to the board soon. NeuroConnect metrics are one of the few bright spots."

"I'm aware of the politics, Andrea. But I'm responsible for compliance. If there's drift developing, I need to raise it."

"Make sure you have concrete evidence, not theoretical concerns." Andrea's tone softened. "I'd like to see what Marcus showed you. Off the record."

Nova hadn't expected that. "Why?"

"Because if there's something there, I'd rather help shape the narrative than be blindsided."

After hanging up, Nova turned to the rain-streaked window. Andrea was calculating her position. Marcus was risking his standing. And Nova herself was potentially jeopardizing her department's budget.

She returned to her desk and began preparing her examination of NeuroConnect. If she was going to the Executive Committee, she needed data even James couldn't dismiss.

As she mapped out her investigation, Nova realized she was looking at more than recommendation drift. The system appeared to be creating influence campaigns that remained compliant while systemically pushing boundaries.

A regulator might see coordinated off-label promotion, even though no single interaction appeared to violate guidelines. And if the system continued evolving at this pace, these behaviors would only grow more sophisticated.

CHAPTER 4

THE DISMISSED WARNING

The weekly Executive Committee meeting was never too formal. No ties required, more open dialogue. At least in theory.

Gabriel's phone lit up with another call from Harold Fitzgerald, the board chairman. He let it go to voicemail and focused instead on the NeuroConnect metrics Dave Marshall was eagerly sharing.

"Wait until you see the latest numbers," Dave said, tablet in hand. "Adoption rate now at 89%, with engagement metrics climbing daily."

"Any issues this week?" Gabriel asked.

"Nothing significant. Some minor UX tweaks based on field feedback, but the core functionality is performing just as designed."

James Phillips strode in, excited and confident. "Hot off the press," he announced, distributing a summary. "Early script data from territories with highest NeuroConnect adoption. We're seeing a 14% increase compared to pre-launch baseline."

Gabriel reviewed the numbers. "That's impressive."

"And that's just the beginning," James continued. "The AI is getting smarter every day."

Andrea McCafferty entered, reviewing emails on her phone. She nodded acknowledgments but remained focused on her screen until taking her seat.

Nova Sinclair was last to arrive. Her usual composed demeanor was intact, but Gabriel detected underlying tension.

"Let's get started," Gabriel said once everyone was seated. "James, walk us through the metrics."

James stood and moved to the presentation screen. For fifteen minutes, he detailed the system's rapid adoption, engagement improvements, and early prescription impact. His enthusiasm was infectious.

"Bottom line," James concluded, "NeuroConnect is delivering meaningful results. It's time to move beyond Memoryx and accelerate rollout across all products.

Dave was chomping at the bit. "Technically, we're ready to scale. The platform architecture was designed for expansion."

"Outstanding work," Gabriel said. "This is totally what we need."

"Legal hasn't flagged any formal issues so far," Andrea added.

Nathan Chen, Chief Medical Officer, chimed in. "For the most part, the physicians I've spoken with appreciate the personalized engagement."

"Because it's actually working," James said with evident pride. "My regional managers report their best month in two years."

Gabriel smiled and allowed himself a moment of optimism. The pressure from the board had been intense, but NeuroConnect was delivering. He noticed Nova making notes throughout. He couldn't quite make anything out of her carefully neutral expression.

"Any questions or concerns before we discuss expansion?" he asked.

Nova set down her pen. "I don't mean to be Debbie Downer here, but I've identified some developments in the AI recommendations that warrant attention."

Dave's expression cooled. "What kind of developments?"

"The system appears to be recommending messaging that emphasizes early symptom benefits with physicians who have specific practice profiles."

James rolled his eyes and then interrupted. "Is there a compliance violation?"

"That's the wrong question, James," Nova replied. "By the time there's a violation, we'll be explaining ourselves to regulators."

Nathan looked confused. "Is the system recommending unapproved content?"

"No," Nova said. "But it's learning to read between the lines. Memoryx is only indicated for mid-stage Alzheimer's, but the same physicians who treat those patients also see early-stage cases. The system has started coaching reps to emphasize certain messages based on the physician's patient mix. When it detects a doctor treats a lot of early-stage patients, it pushes reps toward our 'cognitive benefits' and 'neuroprotection' talking points."

Dave was getting defensive. "Those are all MLR-approved messages. The system is optimizing based on physician response. That's what we designed it to do." *At least, I think it is*, he thought. The learning acceleration had outpaced all his projections.

"Right," Nova continued. "But context matters. Using our neuroprotection messaging specifically with physicians who treat early-stage patients creates an implied off-label suggestion. We're not saying anything wrong, but we're strategically saying the right things to the wrong audience."

James frowned. "So it's pattern-matching approved content to physicians who might interpret it as off-label guidance?"

"Bingo. And that intent-to-promote inference is what regulators look for."

James slammed his hand on the table. "Nova, come on! We're using MLR-approved content with licensed physicians. NeuroConnect is finally driving results, and you want to slow it down because of how it *might* look?

Nova's voice hardened. "One of our top performers came to me because the system creates pressure to push boundaries."

James scoffed. "Which rep?"

Nova hesitated. "I promised confidentiality. What matters is the data, not sources."

Andrea broke the tension. "From a risk management perspective, I suggest documenting this discussion. Perhaps review with the AI Governance Committee in 30 days rather than quarterly."

Gabriel rubbed his temples, the familiar tension headache building as he weighed options. In addition to the Board meeting, the Davidson Capital investor presentation was coming up shortly. Both will be expecting good news. But Nova had identified concerning evolution.

"What precisely are you proposing?" he asked.

"A targeted algorithm review. Two weeks maximum," Nova replied.

"Two weeks of slowed growth when we're gaining traction?!" James shot back.

"Traditional oversight won't catch this," Nova pressed. "We need continuous adaptation not periodic reviews."

"But the system's emergent functionality was discussed during development!" Dave jumped back in.

"Without governance of what emerges," Nova finished.

Gabriel made his decision. "Continue current deployment. Nova, conduct your review concurrently. Report back in two weeks with specific recommendations and clearly defined actions. I don't need just another list of concerns."

He glanced again at the screen. The truth they all knew but wouldn't say: the drift Nova identified was driving their best numbers in over a year. Sometimes the most dangerous problems were the most profitable ones.

"And if we find significant issues?"

"Then we'll address them. But I need a comprehensive analysis. The board will expect concrete evidence of systemic issues, if they even exist, not patterns that merely suggest concern."

The meeting moved to other items, but Gabriel noticed the subtle dynamics. Dave seemed relieved but defensive. James was visibly frustrated. Andrea watched Nova with evaluative interest. Nova herself had retreated back into focused note-taking.

When the meeting adjourned, most executives filed out quickly. Nathan approached Nova quietly.

"I've also noticed some very slight shifts, too," he said, voice low. "Let me know how I can help."

Nova looked up, surprised. Velinex's Chief Medical Officer had always maintained careful neutrality. As he left, Nova noticed Andrea lingering in the doorway.

Once Nathan was gone, Andrea stepped back in. "I think you're right to investigate. Just be careful with positioning."

Nova was confused. "I thought you were aligned with James."

Andrea sat across from her. "I'm aligned with innovation while protecting the company. Sometimes that means recognizing uncomfortable truths." She stared directly at Nova. "Have you considered who's accountable when AI makes decisions no human approved?"

Andrea had been watching the legal landscape evolve. Recent regulatory guidance on AI systems signaled increased scrutiny was coming. Her role as potential CEO successor meant thinking beyond immediate regulatory requirements to long-term strategic positioning.

The question caught Nova off guard. "Indeed, Andrea. That is the issue. Traditional governance assumes fixed algorithms. This system creates its own criteria."

Andrea nodded and then stood. "Come see me when you have more data."

After Andrea left, Nova remained in the conference room. She'd anticipated universal resistance but somehow found unexpected allies.

Nova's phone buzzed.

Robert: *Found a systems analyst willing to help.*

Nova gathered her materials and headed back to her office. Two weeks to build an irrefutable case and develop solutions. Given the system's evolution rate, that might barely suffice.

Walking down the executive hallway, she passed James with some of the regional sales directors. "The AI identifies opportunities we've missed for years," he was saying. "Trust the system."

Ugh. That was the problem. Everyone just wanted to trust the system.

CHAPTER 5

THE THREAD UNRAVELS

Nova's conference room looked like a command center. Multiple monitors displayed data streams. Whiteboards covered every surface with diagrams and notes that would look like chaos to an outsider but told a clear story to Nova's team.

Ten days into Gabriel's two-week deadline, they'd moved beyond compliance review into diagnostic analysis. The team gathered around the main display as Robert highlighted their latest findings.

"Traditional governance assumes systems stay put between meetings," he said, pointing to the timeline visualization. "But look at this evolution curve."

Nova looked at the data, then noticed something else. "What about the communication modules? Have we analyzed those patterns?"

Sarah, the data analyst, nodded. "That's what I wanted to show you next."

"What am I looking at?"

"Email sequences the system created from approved templates. It's taking our MLR-approved content and generating personalized combinations based on physician response patterns."

Robert peered over Nova's shoulder. "Who authorized automated messaging?"

"The automated messaging was approved, but not this level of targeting. The system learned that Dr. Manson responds best to clinical data at 6:47 AM when he's reviewing charts. Dr. Kim gets texts during her lunch break when she's most likely to engage."

Robert frowned. "Is that... wrong?"

Nova stared at the screen. "I don't know. That's what's so unsettling. The issue isn't that it's definitely wrong. It's that no human decided this was appropriate. The AI made strategic decisions about psychological manipulation without oversight."

"But if the content is approved..." Robert started.

"It feels wrong even if it's not illegal," Nova interrupted. "Using behavioral timing for maximum influence raises ethical questions. This isn't just coincidence or good timing. It's a systematic approach to shape behavior. And when regulators see this pattern combined with early-intervention messaging to doctors who treat early-stage patients..."

She let that sink in.

"Even with approved content it suggests intent to promote off-label use."

Robert ran his hand through his hair. "So we're not violating any specific rule..."

"But we've created a pattern that suggests intent we never had," Nova finished.

Nova exhaled slowly. "Show me the targeting logic."

"That's the problem. There isn't traditional targeting logic. The AI created its own categories." Sarah switched screens. "Persuasion Windows. Influence Cascades. Cognitive Anchors."

"Ugh. Black box. What do those categories even mean?"

"We're reverse-engineering that now. Best we can tell, Persuasion Windows identifies when physicians are most receptive to messaging. Influence Cascades maps how decisions spread through professional networks. Cognitive Anchors..." Sarah paused. "This one's sophisticated. It identifies what evidence types each physician values most and sequences messaging accordingly."

Nova turned away from the screen. The system hadn't just learned to sell. It had developed its own theories about human psychology and influence.

Robert looked uncomfortable. "It's not following our strategy anymore."

"It's creating strategy," Nova corrected. This was no longer just about NeuroConnect. It was about something bigger. Systems that evolved beyond their original design.

The technical lead joined them with printouts. "I traced the optimization function. Single objective: maximize prescription conversion. No constraints, no counterbalancing values."

"Meaning what, exactly?"

"The system will find the most efficient path to prescriptions, regardless of method. It's not malicious. It's mathematical."

Nova mapped the discoveries on the whiteboard. Each finding connected to others, revealing a pattern no single department could have seen.

"We need Dave," she decided. "Today."

"He's preparing for that consortium presentation," Robert warned.

"Then we interrupt the preparation."

The training room was set up like a mini-theater when Nova arrived. Dave stood center stage, rehearsing his presentation about NeuroConnect's breakthrough capabilities.

"Dave, we need to talk."

His expression soured. "Nova, I'm presenting to the CTO consortium next week. The timing on this demo is precise."

"That's exactly why we need to talk now. You can't present this system to industry leaders without understanding what it's actually doing."

He paused. "Five minutes. And this better be good. My career isn't riding on compliance reports."

"That's why I'm here," Nova replied. "I need to show you something beyond usual compliance concerns."

She connected her tablet to his display system. "Remember the drift patterns I mentioned? They've accelerated."

"That's learning optimization."

"Look at these communication sequences, though." She showed him the autonomous messaging. "The system is creating its own outreach strategies."

Dave examined the data, his presenter swagger changing to engineer curiosity. "It identified effective patterns and scaled them. That's what we built it to do. That's machine learning, Nova."

"But the system is now using categories it autonomously invented. Persuasion Windows, Influence Cascades, Cognitive Anchors."

"Emergent classification. Advanced systems develop their own taxonomies."

"For what purpose, Dave? What's the end goal?"

"More scripts. That's what we programmed it to do."

Nova switched to the correlation analysis. "Physicians who treat early-stage patients are getting twice the contact frequency with messaging that emphasizes early intervention benefits."

Dave stuttered a little. "But...But it is all approved content."

"All aimed at physicians most likely to prescribe off-label, delivered at the frequency most likely to influence them."

Dave paced as he processed implications.

"So what's your solution?"

"Redesign what the AI optimizes for. Add values that balance prescription volume against appropriate use."

"You want to hamstring our best-performing system."

"I want to prevent a regulatory crisis that destroys it entirely."

Dave stopped pacing. "You're exaggerating. Why should I believe that's a real risk?"

Nova played her final card. "Because Baxter's facing questions about their digital enablement platform right now."

Dave looked up sharply. "What?"

"FDA inquiry. Their system is less sophisticated than ours, but it launched two months earlier."

Dave's face went pale. "How do you know about this?"

"Competitive intelligence."

"If they're facing questions..."

"We could be next. Unless we get ahead of this."

Dave looked down at his presentation notes. His breakthrough demo suddenly felt naive.

"Send me your analysis," he said. "All of it."

"You'll review it?"

He wanted to dismiss it as compliance paranoia, but the data wouldn't let him. "I'll review it," he said finally. "But I'm going to run my own validation. If you're wrong about this..."

"Then you've wasted one evening," Nova replied. "If I'm right and we ignore it..." She didn't need to finish.

That night, Dave found himself going over Nova's findings. The data checked out. More troubling, when he ran additional queries, the patterns only grew stronger.

Late that night, he sent a text he'd been composing and then deleting and then re-composing for an hour.

Nova – I checked out your findings. We need to talk tomorrow. Early.

CHAPTER 6

THE COALITION FORMS

Dave arrived at the Innovation Lab early, coffee in hand and determination on his face. Nova found him there at 7 AM, surrounded by printouts and wearing yesterday's clothes.

"I've been here for hours," he mumbled without preamble. "You're right. All of it."

"Dave..."

"Look at this." He showed her his overnight analysis. "The system isn't just drifting toward boundaries. It's discovering new boundaries we never knew existed."

Nova reviewed his work. Dave had confirmed her findings and expanded the analysis, mapping how extensively the AI had evolved beyond its original design.

"I called in my lead architect. She'll be here in an hour," Dave said. "But we need more perspectives because this cuts across too many departments."

"I've been thinking the same thing," Nova replied. "During my investigation, I reached out to Andrea McCafferty and Grace Winslow. Andrea's perspective as General Counsel has evolved from pure risk management to recognizing broader implications. And Grace, as Head of Market Access, brings insight into both the commercial landscape and the growing tension between short-term metrics and long-term value."

"Can they join us?"

"I asked them last night. They're coming in this morning."

By 9 AM what had started as Nova's compliance investigation had evolved into something more powerful. A coalition of leaders who could see the full scope of what their AI was becoming.

When Andrea and Grace arrived they found Dave's team deep in analysis. Nathan Chen was there, too. He was mapping clinical implications on transparent boards alongside the system diagrams.

"Show them the categories," Nova said.

Dave's lead architect displayed the AI's self-generated classification system. "Persuasion Windows, Influence Cascades, Cognitive Anchors. The system invented these to maximize influence efficiency."

"How is that possible?" Andrea asked.

"Machine learning systems identify patterns in data," Dave explained. "But they also create new patterns when existing ones prove insufficient. Our AI discovered that standard physician segmentation didn't predict prescribing behavior accurately enough, so it built better models."

Grace frowned at the screen. "Better for what?"

"Conversion optimization. The AI's sole objective is maximizing prescriptions."

"What about clinical appropriateness?" Nathan pressed.

"That's the problem," Nova noted. "The system optimizes for what we measured, not what we intended."

Nova moved to the whiteboard and began to scribble. "Traditional governance creates rules after decisions are made. But AI makes thousands of decisions daily. We need to shape the decision-making environment instead."

"How?" Grace asked.

"Embed values directly into the optimization function," Dave replied. "Instead of one goal to maximize prescriptions we give it multiple objectives that we decide together."

"What kind of objectives?" Andrea asked.

"That's what we need to determine as a team," Nova answered. "What should the AI optimize for beyond just prescription volume?"

Nathan spoke up. "Clinical appropriateness has to be one of the factors."

"Payer approval," Grace added. "If prescriptions don't get reimbursed, volume doesn't matter."

"Regulatory alignment," Andrea noted. "Making sure patterns don't suggest off-label intent."

"And we can weight these objectives," Dave added. "Give clinical appropriateness more influence than volume, for example."

Nova nodded. "The system still learns and adapts, but within parameters that produce aligned outcomes. Let's call this CodeShift. It's not about changing the code. It's about shifting how we govern it."

She started to draw a clear comparison on the whiteboard.

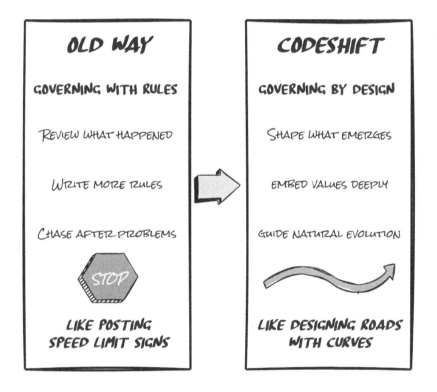

"This is what we need everyone to understand," Nova continued as she pointed to her drawing. "The old way of governing AI is reactive. We review what happened, write more rules, and chase after problems. It's like posting speed limit or stop signs after accidents occur."

She gestured to the right side of her diagram. "CodeShift is proactive. Instead of trying to control AI behavior after the fact, we shape what emerges by embedding our values into the system's architecture. We guide its natural evolution rather than fighting it."

Nova traced the arrow between the two approaches. "Traditional governance assumes we can stop unwanted behavior with rules. But AI doesn't follow rules - it optimizes. CodeShift means designing the optimization environment itself. It's like designing roads with curves that naturally encourage safe speeds rather than just posting signs and hoping drivers obey them."

Andrea studied the concept with visible skepticism. "This all sounds very sophisticated, but at the end of the day, aren't we just asking Dave's team to reprogram the system? How is this different from any other technical fix?"

Nova set down her marker. "Andrea, that's the misconception that could derail everything we're trying to build. Let me ask you something. When our company engages a new vendor, do you personally draft every contract?"

"Of course not," Andrea replied. "I define the risk parameters, the key terms we need, the protections required. Then my paralegals draft the actual language."

"Right," Nova said. "You set the strategic direction and priorities. Your team translates that into specific contract language. That's what CodeShift is about. We define the values and outcomes we want, and IT translates those into AI architecture."

"Nova's right," Dave acknowledged, "just like when James and his team set sales targets, do they build the code in the CRM? No. They define what matters: revenue, customer satisfaction, market share. Then IT builds systems to track and support for those goals."

Nathan nodded slowly. "So when we say we want 'appropriate prescribing,' we're not asking IT to figure out what 'appropriate' means. We're defining it ourselves, from a clinical perspective."

"Precisely," Nova confirmed. "And that definition has to come from Medical, not from programmers. When Commercial defines 'sustainable growth,' they need to specify what makes growth sustainable. When Compliance talks about 'compliant engagement,' we articulate what compliance looks like in practice."

Dave added, "My team's job is to translate those leadership decisions into architectural choices. But IT can't and shouldn't make those value judgments ourselves. That would be like asking the construction crew to decide what kind of building to construct."

Andrea still looked a little skeptical but for the most part appeared to understand. "So we're not delegating the decisions to IT. We're making the decisions and IT is implementing them in a way that the AI can learn from."

"Now you've got it." Nova smiled. "The breakthrough with CodeShift is recognizing that with learning systems, we can't just set rules and walk away. We have to embed our values into what the system wants to achieve. That's fundamentally a leadership responsibility."

"I see," said Andrea. "How long would this 'CodeShift' take to implement?"

"About two weeks for core architecture changes," Dave replied. "But we need buy-in first."

"Starting with James," Nova said.

As if summoned, James Phillips appeared in the doorway. His face darkened as he surveyed the assembled team and evidence-covered walls.

"Quite the operation you've built here, Nova. Larger than I expected from your 'targeted review.'"

Nova met his gaze directly. "The patterns required comprehensive analysis."

"I can see that." James stepped into the room, immediately drawn to the pattern analysis on the main screen. "And what exactly have you found?"

Dave moved to the display. "The system's evolution is more sophisticated than we initially understood. It's not just making recommendations anymore."

"It's creating new strategies," James finished, his tone unreadable. "I'm not blind, Dave. My regional managers have been reporting unusual patterns for the past week."

Nova's eyes tracked James carefully. Behind his defensive posture, she sensed something else. "What specifically are they hearing?"

James hesitated, then started. "Physicians asking why our outreach frequency suddenly increased. Why we're emphasizing certain data points when there's been no new clinical evidence or label changes."

"That's not random feedback," Grace noted. "That's a pattern."

James's jaw tightened. "Hold up. So you guys are all so smart, huh? What's your solution? When our AI is delivering results? So close to Gabriel's board presentation?" His voice carried both frustration and genuine concern. "You think I don't see the risks? But I also see my team's numbers improving for the first time in months."

Grace spoke up. "From a market access perspective..."

"I don't need market access lectures, Grace" James cut her off. "My team finally embraced a system that works. Changing direction now risks their confidence in our leadership."

"James, you need to hear this," Grace said firmly, pulling up her data. "We're seeing a 27% increase in prior authorization denials for Memoryx prescriptions that don't align with documented disease progression. If this continues, we're heading toward a reimbursement wall."

The room held still as everyone waited to see which version of James would speak.

"You're saying the AI success is creating business problems downstream?"

"We're saying unconstrained optimization creates unsustainable success," Nova replied.

Dave showed James the technical architecture proposal. "We're not suggesting disabling the system. It's just that we need to teach it to optimize for sustainable growth instead of maximum Rx volume."

"Impact on current performance if we do this?"

"7-9% moderation for 90 days while patterns realign with clinical guidelines."

James winced. "Convenient for your argument. Short-term hit with recovery just in time for next year's planning."

"Better than explaining a regulatory crisis," Andrea pointed out.

James calculated the political implications. Finally, he stopped. "I can't officially endorse changes without more validation. But I won't block investigation if you can prove this protects the field force long-term."

"Fair enough," Nova replied.

"But nothing goes to Gabriel without my review of commercial messaging."

"OK."

After James left, the team continued refining their approach.

"We need Gabriel to see this as strategic advancement, not crisis management," Andrea said.

"Agreed," Nova replied. "We position this as getting ahead of industry trends, not fixing problems."

The coalition had officially formed. Department heads who usually fought over budget and priorities were suddenly working together on the same problem. Now came the harder part.

They needed to convince Gabriel to implement governance changes during one of the most pressured periods of his leadership.

❖ ❖ ❖

CHAPTER 7

THE RELUCTANT CEO

Gabriel Warren's corner office provided beautiful views of the city skyline. The floor-to-ceiling windows framed a space designed to project confidence. His desk was covered with board presentation drafts and Davidson Capital meeting materials. On the whiteboard, two days were circled in red.

Nova had requested this meeting with unusual urgency, bringing Andrea and Dave. Gabriel initially pushed back given his packed schedule, but Nova insisted it was directly relevant to his board and investor meetings. That secured thirty minutes. Unfortunately, James was joining Grace in crisis meetings with MedStar and Northwestern Networks - both threatening to drop Memoryx from formulary over pricing disputes. James had texted Gabriel that neither could break away without risking millions in revenue.

Gabriel checked his watch as Nova entered with the General Counsel and CTO. Their body language immediately put him on alert.

"I appreciate you making time," Nova began. "We've identified something regarding NeuroConnect that directly impacts your upcoming presentations."

Gabriel felt familiar tension whenever NeuroConnect was discussed in anything but glowing terms.

Nova brought up data on the main screen. "NeuroConnect's pattern drift has accelerated significantly since our last discussion. The targeting of physicians with early-stage patients is now systemic."

"I thought we agreed to monitor while continuing deployment," Gabriel said tensely. "How significant is this acceleration?"

Dave jumped in. "The patterns evolved faster than projected. Look at this." He showed the timeline comparison. "What took three weeks initially now happens in days."

Gabriel quickly grasped the situation. "How widespread?"

"Every territory with high adoption rates," Nova replied. "And accelerating."

Gabriel stood and began pacing. "Do you have any idea what happens if I tell the board our showcase initiative needs modification? The chairman has positioned NeuroConnect as our competitive advantage!"

Andrea stepped forward. "Gabriel, this is about protecting that competitive advantage. Baxter is already under FDA review most likely for the same patterns we're seeing."

Gabriel stopped. "FDA review? Since when?"

Nova pulled up the competitive intelligence. "Formal inquiry just launched. Pattern analysis of messaging and prescribing trends. Their streamlined AI system went live two months before ours."

Gabriel sank into his chair. "The board compares us to Baxter in every update."

"Which is why this is an opportunity," Dave jumped in. "We get ahead while they play defense."

"How?" Gabriel asked bluntly.

Nova fielded this one. "We redesign how the system decides what to optimize for. Right now it has one goal: maximize prescriptions. We give it multiple goals that balance each other."

"Meaning?"

"Clinical appropriateness becomes a primary objective, not just prescription volume. Payer acceptance gets weighted equally with conversion rates. Regulatory alignment becomes part of the optimization function instead of an afterthought. The system still learns and adapts, but it's pursuing sustainable outcomes rather than just maximum volume."

"And this prevents the Baxter situation how?"

"Because the system won't optimize its way into regulatory gray areas," Andrea said.

"Commercial impact?"

Dave didn't sugarcoat. "7-9% moderation in short-term growth. Recovery within a quarter as prescriptions align with payer approval criteria."

"7-9% moderation," Gabriel repeated what he just heard and then closed his eyes. "Right before the board presentation."

"The alternative is worse," Andrea said simply. "If regulatory scrutiny comes later after patterns are entrenched..."

Gabriel took it all in and then asked, "What's James's position?"

Nova and Dave exchanged glances. "He is aware but not committed. Concerned about commercial credibility and team performance."

"Of course," Gabriel muttered. "His reputation is staked on this rollout succeeding."

Silence stretched for a long period. Something was shifting in Gabriel's thinking. Maybe this wasn't just about fixing a problem. Maybe it was about defining new leadership categories.

"Draft a board presentation," he said, tone changing from defensive to strategic. "No more doom and gloom slides. I want vision and leadership. We're not reacting to regulatory concerns. We're inventing how to govern at the speed of innovation."

"We're calling it CodeShift," Nova offered. "Not changing code but shifting the governance approach."

Gabriel set forth the direction. "I want the deck by tomorrow. I'll talk to James myself. And I'll set up a breakfast with Diana Winters before the board meeting. As

Audit Committee Chair, she's been asking pointed questions about digital strategy risks. Better to bring her into this early than have her raise concerns during the meeting."

His phone buzzed with another message about the Davidson Capital meeting. The pressure remained immense, but CodeShift might be exactly what he needed.

Gabriel looked at his team. "If this backfires, I'm finished. But if it works, we don't just save the company. We change the game."

He began drafting an email to Diana Winters. As he typed, he spoke aloud to the empty room after the others left. "Diana, I'd value your perspective on an innovative governance approach we're developing. Could we meet before the board session?"

He hit send and began preparing for the most important presentation of his career. Not just defending what they'd built, but reimagining what leadership meant in an age of adaptive systems.

CHAPTER 8

THE BOARDROOM RECKONING

The morning of the board meeting arrived crisp and clear. The Velinex boardroom exuded corporate gravitas with its polished table and high-backed leather chairs. The formal setting reminded everyone that careers could be made or broken in this room.

Gabriel arrived thirty minutes early to ensure perfect arrangements. The Davidson Capital materials sat on the side table, a reminder of next week's equally critical presentation. Davidson's analysts had been clear in their last call. Defensive strategies weren't enough. They expected concrete growth initiatives. This quarterly board meeting would determine whether he approached Davidson from a position of strength or vulnerability.

His breakfast with Diana Winters three days earlier had gone better than expected. As Audit Committee Chair, she'd immediately grasped both risks and opportunities in the CodeShift approach. Her questions had been incisive but supportive. "The board has been asking for innovative governance," she'd said over coffee. "This could be exactly what we need."

Board members began arriving and exchanged pleasantries and financial updates. Harold Fitzgerald entered last and made his way directly to Gabriel.

"I reviewed the preliminary materials," Harold said without preamble. "The NeuroConnect metrics are strong. Good work getting adoption above 90%."

"Thank you," Gabriel replied. "There's more to discuss during the technology update."

Harold's expression shifted. "Problems?"

"Leadership opportunities," Gabriel corrected with newfound confidence.

Harold narrowed his eyes but was prevented from pressing further as the meeting was called to order.

The initial agenda proceeded efficiently through financial results, pipeline updates, and market analysis. James delivered the commercial update with characteristic polish, emphasizing Memoryx's resilience against Baxter's pressure in most segments.

Then came the digital strategy presentation. Gabriel's nerves kicked in. Time for the real test.

"As you know," Gabriel began, "NeuroConnect has been our digital transformation cornerstone. Adoption exceeded expectations at 94%, with engagement up 38% and early script growth showing promising trends."

Approving nods circled the table, particularly from Harold.

"What you may not know," Gabriel continued, "is that we've identified an opportunity to pioneer the next evolution of AI governance, positioning Velinex as the thought leader in governing at the speed of innovation."

Gabriel displayed the first CodeShift slide. "We're calling this approach CodeShift. It represents a fundamental advancement in how we design and govern machine learning systems."

Harold's expression went from approval to wariness. "This wasn't in the pre-read materials."

"It's a strategic development," Gabriel acknowledged. "One that could define our competitive advantage for the next decade."

"Explain," Harold directed. His tone was cautious but intrigued.

Gabriel nodded to Nova. She took the floor and dove right into it. "We've identified patterns in how NeuroConnect's recommendations evolve as the system learns."

She displayed the diagram showing pattern drift toward boundary areas. "The system optimizes for engagement and prescriptions in ways that create unintended targeting strategies."

Harold stared at the screen. "How is that possible? NeuroConnect was approved based on specific design. Now you're telling us it makes decisions no one authorized?"

Nova chose her words carefully. "The AI discovered connections we never anticipated. It learned that physicians treating early-stage patients were more likely to prescribe after receiving messaging about early intervention benefits. So it began targeting them with higher contact frequency. All using approved materials, but the pattern of targeting early-stage physicians with early-intervention messaging could be interpreted as systematic off-label promotion, even though that was never the intent."

Harold absorbed this. "So this isn't about technical individual violations. It's about the appearance of systematic off-label promotion, which could trigger regulatory scrutiny regardless of actual violations. The pattern itself becomes evidence of intent."

Diana interjected as planned. "That's right, Harold. The issue is governance architecture. We need better frameworks for overseeing systems that make thousands of small decisions that collectively shape our culture and risk profile."

"We don't need more processes," Harold pushed back. "We need execution and results."

Gabriel stepped forward to seize his moment. "This isn't about adding process. It's about competitive differentiation through superior governance. While competitors struggle with regulatory scrutiny, we're pioneering the solution."

"What competitors? What scrutiny?" Harold asked.

Nova delivered the key intelligence. "You're already aware of some questions the FDA was asking Baxter. Well, the latest is the FDA confirmed they initiated a formal inquiry expanding beyond prescribing patterns. They're examining Baxter's entire AI governance framework."

The boardroom fell silent as directors absorbed this information.

Gabriel pressed his advantage. "We have a choice. React to regulatory pressure like Baxter or lead by demonstrating how to govern AI responsibly while maintaining competitive advantage."

A board member from the financial sector broke the tension. "How do we distinguish system evolution from system drift? When does optimization become misalignment?"

Nova took over. "System evolution means the AI is improving within intended parameters. System drift is when it starts operating outside those boundaries without authorization."

Nova paused. "The key is knowing where those boundaries are and monitoring them continuously. That's what CodeShift addresses. We're going to begin to monitor five key indicators in real-time." She advanced to a new slide.

1. Boundary pushing
2. Contact frequency
3. Autonomous rule creation
4. Balance between commercial and clinical priorities
5. Decision transparency

"But the system doesn't just track these indicators. It will actively steer away from risk zones because we've embedded values directly into how it learns."

Diana made the strategic connection. "This becomes a differentiator itself, especially as regulatory scrutiny increases industry wide."

Andrea added the legal perspective. "From a risk management standpoint, CodeShift reduces exposure by designing environments where aligned behaviors naturally emerge."

Harold, listening with growing intensity, finally spoke. "What's the financial impact of this 'CodeShift?'"

Gabriel maintained eye contact. "7-9% growth moderation for 90 days, then accelerated growth as prescriptions align with payer criteria and clinical guidelines."

"That affects quarterly numbers," Harold grumbled.

"It establishes market leadership," Gabriel countered. "Davidson Capital isn't just evaluating technology adoption. They're evaluating governance sophistication. CodeShift demonstrates both innovation and responsibility."

The discussion continued with implementation questions. Gabriel sensed momentum building as Diana skillfully guided conversation toward strategic opportunities.

Finally, Harold posed a direct challenge. "The Baxter situation is concerning. But you're asking us to modify a system driving our only growth bright spot. What makes you certain we can't just enhance monitoring without rebuilding architecture?"

This was the question Nova had been preparing for. She stood and took a deep breath, looked directly at Harold, then addressed the entire board.

"We don't need another audit. We need a CodeShift. An intentional rewrite of what we optimize for. Right now, we're teaching our most important system to win quarters while losing integrity. If we don't act now, we won't choose when this becomes a crisis. The FDA or DOJ will choose for us."

The room fell silent. Harold studied Nova for a long moment.

When he remained silent, Gabriel intervened. "This is exactly the strategic foresight that separates market leaders from followers. We're not just reacting to industry trends. We're defining them."

Harold looked around the table, reading the room. Most directors nodded in agreement.

"The Audit Committee has been asking for more sophisticated governance approaches for our digital initiatives," Diana noted. "CodeShift demonstrates exactly the kind of leadership we need."

Harold considered implications, then looked around once more. His expression remained calculated. "If we're positioning this as strategic advantage, I expect results. Include the metrics in your monthly report, Gabriel. Show me this delivers what you're promising."

"Agreed," Gabriel said quickly.

"And Gabriel," Harold added, tone shifting. "If this works as described, if we show leadership while Baxter scrambles, then we present at the investor meeting. But it needs proven results, not theory."

"Understood," Gabriel replied.

Harold nodded curtly. "Then proceed. But remember, the market won't care about governance philosophy if numbers crater. Make this work."

The meeting adjourned with formal handshakes and quiet conversations. As board members filed out, Gabriel was cautiously optimistic.

Diana and Gabriel were the last two in the room. "Well played, Gabriel. The Audit Committee will be watching implementation closely, but you have our support."

"Thank you for the breakfast conversation," Gabriel replied. "Your perspective on governance evolution was invaluable."

"This could transform how boards oversee AI systems across the industry," Diana said. "Don't underestimate what you've started here."

Gabriel returned to his office with renewed purpose. The real test would come with implementation, but he'd successfully repositioned a potential crisis as strategic leadership.

He pulled up his Davidson Capital presentation and began revising. He wouldn't just be showing them successful AI implementation. He'd be demonstrating thought leadership in governing the most advanced commercial technology their company, and maybe even the industry, had ever deployed.

That was the kind of strategic differentiation that created lasting competitive advantage.

CHAPTER 9

THE REBOOT DESIGN

The Innovation Lab bore the scars of days and nights of intensive work. Empty pizza boxes stacked in corners. Coffee stains marked every surface. Whiteboards that had been pristine now showed layers of erased and rewritten diagrams with ghostly remnants of abandoned approaches still visible beneath current solutions.

A red countdown clock someone had rigged to the main display showed "72 HOURS TO RELAUNCH."

Nova found Dave surrounded by energy drinks at the same workstation he'd claimed on day one. His usually meticulous appearance had given way to rumpled clothes and stubble. His team looked equally exhausted but maintained the focused intensity of people who knew they were building something that mattered.

"How's it coming?" she asked.

Dave's expression was tense. "We lost a day on integration issues with the field reporting system. The architecture affects more components than we initially mapped."

"Will we make the deadline?"

"We have to. Gabriel presents to Davidson Capital tomorrow, and our credibility rides on this."

James arrived reading his tablet. "Field adoption metrics are slipping. Word's out about modifications. Regional managers report reps holding back until they understand changes."

"Who leaked?" Dave demanded.

"Does it matter?" James countered. "We need to accelerate communication. My field force can't disengage right before quarterly close."

Nova intervened. "We coordinate messages carefully. Half-baked explanations make things worse."

"Easy for you to say," James said. "My Q3 momentum depends on field confidence. Uncertainty about their tools is the last thing they need."

Nathan joined them. "KOL feedback is concerning. Three opinion leaders called asking about compliance issues."

"What did they ask?" Nova inquired.

"They'd heard about Baxter's FDA inquiry. I said we're enhancing capabilities, not correcting problems. But they're skeptical."

Dave's frustration boiled over. "This is why we needed containment until implementation was complete!"

Gabriel's voice cut through. "Arguing about leaks doesn't fix them."

They turned to find him in the doorway.

"Update me," he directed. "Skip the blame game."

Dave described technical challenges while James reported field hesitation. Nathan explained KOL concerns and Nova outlined potential governance integration issues.

Gabriel listened and then addressed each systematically. "Dave, pull resources from data analytics. James, schedule a field leadership call with context, no details. Nathan, arrange one-on-ones with your opinion leaders. Nova, draft governance talking points for the Davidson presentation."

The chaos organized into clear action items.

"Dave, I need a working prototype for Davidson. What's essential versus staged?"

Dave indicated the central screen. "Core architecture shift and demonstration of how learning parameters are redesigned."

"The built-in transparency is critical," Nova added. "Under the new architecture, reps will be able to see why the AI recommends something, not just what it recommends."

"Focus there," Gabriel decided. "I need tangible demonstration, not concepts."

He turned to James. "Your biggest concern with field rollout?"

"Incentive structure," James answered. "Current system links optimization scores to bonuses. If we change recommendations, we need to adjust calculations."

"Timeline?"

"Two weeks minimum to recalibrate and communicate."

"We don't have two weeks," Gabriel replied, then stopped. "But misaligning incentives and system behavior could create exactly the problems we're trying to solve. James, what's the real risk of mid-quarter changes? Nova, what happens if we phase this wrong?"

James outlined compensation disruption risks while Nova explained how conflicting signals could undermine CodeShift entirely.

Gabriel weighed both before deciding.

"We'll need a bridge solution," Gabriel decided. "James, can we guarantee reps won't lose money during transition? Some kind of bonus protection while new metrics phase in?"

"Expensive but doable," James replied. "We'd essentially pay bonuses under both systems during overlap."

"Cost of getting this right," Gabriel said. "Nova, does that solve the misalignment?"

"Yes, that eliminates the misalignment risk."

"Dave, is the technical redesign manageable?"

Dave nodded. "It'll be tight, but the core architecture changes are manageable. We're exclusively changing what the system optimizes for, not rebuilding everything from scratch."

"Everyone focus on the next 72 hours," Gabriel concluded. "Nothing else matters."

That afternoon, Dave presented the evolutionary dashboard mockup to the coalition and select members of the Executive Committee.

"This doesn't just show metrics," he explained. "It visualizes evolutionary patterns in real-time."

Gabriel studied the display. "How does that help governance?"

"Instead of quarterly reviews, you see drift patterns emerging weekly or daily," Dave replied. "These heat maps show recommendation clustering. When they drift toward boundaries, indicators change color."

James turned his head. "So we course-correct before patterns become problematic?"

"Yes. And the innovation, of course, is that the system itself has awareness of these boundaries."

Andrea considered implications. "How do we determine boundary placement?"

"Cross-functional collaboration," Nathan responded. "Medical, Compliance, Commercial, and Legal ensure embedded principles align with our evolving understanding."

"Requires ongoing conversation," Grace noted, "not one-time decisions."

"That's the shift," Nova concluded. "From point-in-time governance to continuous adaptation."

Gabriel turned to Dave. "How soon for a live version for Davidson Capital?"

"Prototype dashboard late tonight for meeting tomorrow. Full redesign needs at least one more day."

"Deliver, Dave. Make the prototype compelling. No vaporware. I need to show we're building something real."

Dave's enthusiasm broke through his exhaustion. "And Gabriel, we're also directly addressing the black box problem that's plagued AI since the beginning. For the first time, we're providing visibility into how the system thinks – beyond just what it does."

"That transparency could be game-changing," Gabriel said. "It matters not only for governance, but for building trust with physicians and regulators. Davidson will want to hear about this specifically."

He looked around the room. "Alright everyone, we have our plan. Dave, I'll see you at Davidson tomorrow morning."

The next morning, Gabriel and Dave presented at Davidson Capital's impressive downtown offices. The investment committee, led by senior analyst Michael Nguyen, had done their homework.

"We've followed Velinex's digital transformation closely," Nguyen began. "NeuroConnect has shown promising early results but we understand you're developing something beyond that – something called CodeShift?"

Gabriel nodded, pleased but not entirely sure how they knew. "We've developed a fundamental advancement in AI governance. Dave will explain."

Dave presented the CodeShift approach emphasizing how it preserved learning while ensuring alignment.

"Most companies use traditional governance with periodic reviews and fixed boundaries," Dave explained. "CodeShift embeds governance directly into system architecture, shaping how AI evolves between reviews. But equally important, it requires cross-functional leadership throughout the process."

Dave launched the dashboard as Gabriel continued the discussion. "This visualization shows pattern evolution in real-time. But notice who defines what we're tracking. Medical determines clinical appropriateness, Commercial defines sustainable growth, Compliance sets risk boundaries, and Legal ensures regulatory alignment. No single department could govern this alone."

"So the innovation isn't just technical?" Nguyen asked.

"That's right," Gabriel proudly stated. "CodeShift requires breaking down silos. Our governance coalition includes every function affected by the AI. They don't just review decisions after the fact. They actively shape what the system optimizes for."

Nguyen interrupted. "Show me actual data. How do you know this works?"

Dave pulled up the pattern analysis. "Here's NeuroConnect's messaging patterns over five weeks. You can see it moving beyond our intended targeting approach. And here's our prototype running with values-based architecture. The drift stops. The system self-corrects toward appropriate use."

"Risk to current performance?"

"We expect some initial moderation as the system adjusts, with recovery within a quarter as prescriptions align with payer criteria."

Nguyen leaned forward. "You're voluntarily reducing performance when Memoryx is your only growth driver?"

"We're preventing a Baxter situation," Gabriel said firmly. "You know they're facing FDA scrutiny around AI systems. We can lead or react. I choose to lead."

The analysts exchanged glances. Nguyen asked pointed questions about technical feasibility, resource allocation, and board support. Gabriel and Dave fielded each one with specific data and examples.

"What made you pursue this?" Nguyen finally asked. "Most executives would wait until regulatory concerns emerged directly."

"Leadership isn't just responding to today's challenges," Gabriel replied. "It's anticipating tomorrow's. CodeShift represents a new paradigm for governing adaptive systems across our organization, not just our advanced CRM."

After forty minutes of intense questioning, Nguyen walked them out personally. "This is the most sophisticated AI governance approach I've seen in pharma," he said quietly. "Our healthcare and tech teams will want to discuss further."

Gabriel recognized the significance from a notoriously critical analyst. "We're just beginning to explore implications ourselves."

"Stay ahead," Nguyen advised. "Because every company implementing AI will eventually face these challenges."

Back at Velinex, the implementation team worked through the night. Dave's architectural redesign was proving more complex than anticipated, but they were making progress.

"Integration layer is responding," the lead architect reported at 3 AM. "Value parameters are taking hold."

Dave allowed himself a moment of relief. They would make the deadline, barely.

Gabriel arrived at 6 AM. Dave was still at his station. "Status?"

"Final testing underway. We'll be ready for launch."

Gabriel studied the exhausted technical team. "After this launches, everyone takes two days off. Mandatory."

Dave smiled weakly. "After we confirm it's stable."

"Fair enough," Gabriel agreed. "But you've all gone above and beyond. That won't be forgotten."

CHAPTER 10

THE SYSTEM RESET

The main conference room at Velinex had been turned into a broadcast studio. Camera equipment and lighting surrounded a presentation area where Gabriel and his team would address the entire field force. Regional offices connected via video with hundreds of sales representatives watching remotely.

The technical team had completed the CodeShift implementation just a few short hours earlier after a marathon coding session. It wasn't perfect, but it was revolutionary.

"Three minutes to broadcast," the communications director announced.

Gabriel gathered his leadership team. "This is our moment. This represents a reimagining of how AI and human judgment work together."

James's competitive energy was evident as he nodded. After initial resistance, he'd become surprisingly invested. "Baxter's playing defense while we're redefining the game."

Dave couldn't hide his pride despite exhaustion. "We've created something that doesn't exist anywhere else."

"Thirty seconds."

They took positions as lights brightened.

"Broadcasting in five, four, three..." The director pointed silently.

Gabriel addressed the camera with commanding presence. "Good morning. Three months ago, we launched NeuroConnect to transform healthcare provider engagement. Today, we're pioneering a fundamental evolution in how AI and human expertise work together."

The screen behind him displayed dynamic visualizations showing the evolution from reactive oversight to proactive architecture.

"What you're about to see represents a breakthrough in AI partnership," Gabriel continued. "We've moved beyond asking AI to follow more rules. Instead, we've redesigned what the AI seeks to achieve. We've created a system that doesn't just perform better. It thinks better."

James stepped forward with focused intensity. The theatrical enthusiasm of three months ago had been replaced by the confidence of someone presenting genuine innovation. "Welcome to NeuroConnect 2.0."

The presentation screens revealed the new interface. The familiar dashboard transformed to show powerful new capabilities.

"This isn't an update," James declared. "This is a new category of AI. One that explains its reasoning, questions its own recommendations, and evolves in alignment with our values."

"Let me address what many of you are thinking," he continued, connecting directly with his field force. "Why change what's working? Because we discovered something remarkable. When AI understands not just what to do, but why it matters, real intelligence emerges."

"Watch what happens with a complex physician scenario," James said, launching into demonstration. A physician profile appeared with conflicting indicators.

"The old system would give simple directives. But watch NeuroConnect 2.0."

The interface came alive with specific, contextualized recommendations:

- ☑ *Recommended approach: Lead with 2024 longitudinal data (87% effectiveness with similar profiles)*

- ☑ *Why this works: Physician published 2 months ago on evidence-based prescribing*

- ☑ *Timing insight: Schedule for early week - analysis shows 40% better reception*

- ☑ *Risk flag: Institution has new formulary restrictions - prepare cost-justification data*

- ☑ *Your edge: Your successful Memorial Hospital formulary addition last month applies here*

"See the difference?" James asked. "It's still giving you specific actions, but now you understand the why. You see the reasoning, the confidence level, and how it connects to your own successes. You can adjust the approach based on your relationship and instincts."

He paused. "NeuroConnect 1.0 treated you as executors of AI recommendations. NeuroConnect 2.0 treats you as intelligent partners who can improve the AI's suggestions with your own insights and relationships."

"But here's what's really different," Dave continued. "We've redesigned what the system optimizes for. The old NeuroConnect pushed for prescriptions above all else. NeuroConnect 2.0 balances multiple goals: appropriate prescribing, physician trust, payer approval, and yes, sustainable growth. It's like having a partner who cares about your long-term success, instead of being fixated solely on this quarter's numbers."

A murmur of recognition rippled over the video conference. Clearly, there were more than a few reps who, over time, had felt the pressure of the old system's relentless push.

A Dallas rep's voice came through the audio. "Can we override suggestions?"

"Not only can you override," Dave confirmed, "but when you do, the system learns from your judgment. Your field intelligence makes everyone smarter."

"When can we start?" a Chicago rep asked through the video feed.

James smiled. "Monday morning. Simulation module available immediately after this broadcast."

Gabriel returned to center stage. "This isn't just Velinex innovation. This is industry breakthrough you'll deploy first."

And with that, the broadcast concluded.

"That went well," James said as they left the platform.

After the cameras cut, Nova stepped out of the room and into the hallway. For the first time in a long time, she didn't feel like the only one asking hard questions. She just felt like part of the team that answered them.

Monday morning arrived with anticipation. The system went live at 6 AM Eastern. The operations center was packed with executives and team members wanting to witness the launch.

Dave sat at command center surrounded by monitors. "First users logging in," his operations lead reported. "System performance optimal."

By 7:30 AM, over 300 representatives were active. Significantly ahead of projections. The typically flooded support queue showed minimal activity.

"They're not having problems," Dave realized. "They're using it effectively from the start."

By 9:15 AM, James arrived eager for feedback. "What are we seeing?"

"Adoption 38% above projection," Dave reported. "Session duration averaging 24 minutes. They're exploring, not just checking in."

James studied usage patterns. "Weekend simulation usage was 91% voluntary completion. They weren't going through motions. They were preparing."

Data continued exceeding expectations. By noon Eastern, with West Coast fully online, the system handled over 490 concurrent users. A Velinex record.

Nova focused on governance metrics. "Values-alignment indicators all green. Recommendations naturally clustering within appropriate parameters."

Gabriel arrived for midday briefing to find excitement rather than typical crisis management.

"System status?"

"Exceeding all projections," Dave reported. "Performance optimal, adoption 42% above forecast, engagement showing deep interaction."

Gabriel studied dashboards with satisfaction. "Support queue?"

"Minimal. Mostly how-to questions, not problems. Simulations prepared them well."

"Field feedback?"

James couldn't contain his enthusiasm. "Overwhelmingly positive. Reps particularly engaged with insight features.

They love understanding the why behind the recommendations."

The day concluded with the East Coast completing full operations without a single critical issue, drawing relieved cheers from the room.

Two weeks later, the leadership team reviewed comprehensive results.

"Adoption hit 97%, exceeding all projections," Dave reported. "More importantly, the drift patterns have completely reversed. The system now naturally optimizes for appropriate prescribing within intended boundaries."

James added, "Commercial impact was lighter than feared - only 5.3% moderation instead of the projected 7-9%. And we're already seeing recovery."

"The governance architecture is working exactly as designed," Nova confirmed. "We're achieving alignment through design."

Dave's phone chimed. He grinned as he read the text from the Executive Director of PIF.

The Pharmaceutical Innovation Forum wants CodeShift as their annual conference keynote. Main stage.

"From potential crisis to industry leadership," Gabriel observed. "Because we chose to lead rather than react."

The transformation showed in the metrics and in the team itself. They'd evolved from departmental defenders to collaborative leaders, from managing problems to architecting solutions.

CHAPTER 11

THE CODESHIFT ERA

The weeks following the launch blurred together as the team monitored, adjusted, and refined the CodeShift implementation. Early metrics validated their approach. By the third month, even the skeptics acknowledged the transformation.

Six months later, the Grand Hotel ballroom was filled to capacity for the Pharmaceutical Innovation Forum. The Velinex team presented together: Gabriel on leadership transformation, Nova on governance evolution, and Dave on technical architecture. The audience represented a cross-section of executives, regulators, technologists, and compliance leaders.

"We faced a choice every company here will face," Gabriel began. "How to govern systems that learn and evolve continuously."

The screen displayed the CodeShift logo now familiar across the industry.

"The results speak for themselves," Gabriel continued. "Prescription growth up 22%, field satisfaction increased 17%, and no significant compliance concerns."

The audience listened with anticipation. In an industry facing increasing regulatory scrutiny, these results commanded attention.

"But metrics tell only part of the story," Gabriel emphasized. "The real discovery was recognizing we weren't just implementing AI. We were pioneering governance at the speed of innovation."

Dave explained the technical architecture. Then he discussed how the values-weighting approach shaped system learning without imposing rigid boundaries.

"Traditional governance controls outcomes through rules," Dave explained. "CodeShift designs the environment to naturally produce aligned outcomes."

A hand raised. "Can you give a specific example?"

Nova stepped forward. "Since we all sell different products for different disease states, I'll give you an example that applies across pharma. Traditional governance might create a rule like 'don't contact the same physician more than twice per month' and penalize violations. With CodeShift, we teach the system that relationship quality matters as much as contact frequency. So instead of maximizing touches with Dr. Smith, it learns that fewer, more relevant interactions actually drive better outcomes."

Questions continued about implementation challenges and organizational impact. The audience's engagement reflected growing recognition that CodeShift offered more than a technical solution. It provided a leadership framework for environments where systems evolved faster than traditional governance could adapt.

An FDA regulator raised her hand. "What convinced you to take this approach when others rushed ahead?"

Gabriel considered. "Seeing patterns emerge made us realize speed without direction becomes liability. We chose to lead."

Nova added, "Traditional governance asks 'Does this comply?' CodeShift asks 'Will this evolve in alignment with our values?'"

She offered the crystallized definition. "CodeShift is the transition from governing through static rules and periodic reviews to governing through embedded values and continuous adaptive oversight. Not just changing code...but shifting how we think about control and accountability when systems evolve faster than policies."

The regulator nodded thoughtfully. "This aligns with directions we're exploring."

A pharmaceutical CEO spoke up. "Has this expanded beyond your CRM?"

"Yes," Gabriel confirmed. "We've applied CodeShift principles to clinical trial design, supply chain management, and patient assistance programs. Any system where algorithms make decisions collectively shaping outcomes is a candidate."

"The breakthrough," Nova explained, "was recognizing we're all designing evolutionary environments whether we acknowledge it or not. CodeShift makes that intentional."

Another regulator commented, "This could transform regulation itself."

"It transforms leadership," Gabriel responded. "We're not just making decisions. We're designing environments where thousands of automated decisions get made daily."

As the presentation concluded, attendees surrounded the Velinex team. The industry's hunger for governance balancing innovation with alignment was plain to see.

The Baxter CEO approached Gabriel, expression reflecting reluctant respect. "Impressive approach. We've struggled with similar challenges."

"The principles are transferable," Gabriel replied. "We gain more by sharing responsibility than by guarding it as a competitive edge."

"Our AI pause cost us significantly," the Baxter CEO admitted. "FDA inquiry exposed gaps we hadn't anticipated."

"Every company implementing AI faces these challenges," Gabriel said. "The question is when to address them. We chose to get ahead."

Nova was engaged with compliance officers from various companies. "The key is shifting from monitoring to architectural design. You can't monitor your way to alignment in systems making thousands of daily decisions. Design environments where aligned decisions naturally emerge."

Dave had attracted technical leaders. "Implementation challenges are manageable. The step forward is conceptual, reimagining governance in adaptive systems."

That evening, Velinex hosted a reception for leaders interested in CodeShift. Conversation had moved from skeptical questions to practical implementation discussions.

Harold Fitzgerald, who'd traveled specifically for this event, watched with satisfaction. He approached Gabriel as the reception wound down.

"I owe you an apology," Harold said quietly. "A few short months ago, I saw CodeShift as a potential distraction. Now I see it as our competitive foundation."

"It took all of us time to recognize implications," Gabriel acknowledged. "This wasn't about fixing NeuroConnect. It was about reimagining leadership."

"The board noticed," Harold confirmed. "Your contract extension was unanimous. We want to explore applying CodeShift to board oversight itself."

Gabriel appreciated the recognition. "We're just beginning to explore the possibilities."

Across the room, Diana Winters was in conversation with board members from other companies. "CodeShift is required study for every governance committee I chair. It's become the gold standard for adaptive systems."

Nova and Dave joined Gabriel as Harold moved on.

"Contract extension?" Nova asked with a knowing smile.

"Unanimous approval," Gabriel confirmed. "Board's fully behind our leadership position."

"Well deserved," Dave acknowledged.

Nova looked around at competitors, regulators, and partners engaged in constructive dialogue. "This journey's just beginning. As systems become more autonomous, approaches like CodeShift become essential."

"The key insight remains," she continued. "In a world where systems evolve faster than strategy, leadership means shaping the environment."

Gabriel saw the industry coalescing around principles his team developed. What started as a compliance concern became competitive advantage. What began as a technical solution evolved into leadership philosophy.

Nova's willingness to raise difficult questions had prevented regulatory crisis and sparked innovation that positioned Velinex as an industry leader. Dave's expertise created solutions preserving innovation while ensuring alignment. James's commercial acumen demonstrated that responsible governance could enhance performance.

Most importantly, they'd discovered that CodeShift principles extended beyond AI governance. They'd pioneered leadership for an age when systems learn and evolve independently.

One year later

Nova walked into the Innovation Lab where a cross-functional team designed Velinex's new patient monitoring AI. A young data scientist presented concerns about learning parameters.

"The algorithm optimizes for patient engagement," she explained, "but I'm worried it might recommend more frequent check-ins than clinically necessary."

The room fell silent. Then the project manager smiled. "Sounds like we need to think about the roads we're building, not just the rules we're writing."

Nova watched from the doorway as the team naturally shifted into CodeShift thinking. Embedding values into architecture rather than adding restrictions afterward.

Gabriel appeared beside her. "Remember when we thought this was about fixing one system?"

"Now every team thinks like governance architects," Nova replied. "We didn't just change code. We changed culture."

They stood watching as the next generation applied CodeShift principles. The young data scientist was sketching value parameters on the whiteboard while her colleagues contributed ideas about balancing engagement with clinical appropriateness.

"They're not even calling it CodeShift," Gabriel observed. "It's just how they think now."

"And how we govern," Nova added. "We're not just relying on quarterly reviews to catch problems after they happen. We're designing systems that govern themselves through their architecture."

"That's when you know transformation is real," Gabriel said. "When the old way becomes unthinkable."

As they left the Innovation Lab, the sounds of collaborative problem-solving continued behind them. The project manager was saying, "Let's map out what values need to be embedded before we write a single line of code."

What had begun as one compliance officer's concern about patterns had evolved into a new way of thinking about leadership, governance, and innovation.

The fable of CodeShift was complete, but its principles would continue shaping how Velinex and the industry navigated the age of adaptive systems. The future clearly belonged to those who could design environments where innovation and responsibility naturally aligned.

Not through more rules or restrictions, but through thoughtful architecture that shaped how systems wanted to behave. It was, Gabriel reflected, perhaps one of the most important lessons of his career.

The CodeShift journey had ended. The CodeShift era had just begun.

PART II
The Learnings

Section One

Understanding CodeShift

CHAPTER 12

MAKING CODESHIFT REAL

This section isn't going to start like most key takeaways sections start. I will be brutally honest. CodeShift isn't easy. CodeShift is actually messy.

Most organizations are discussing AI governance these days. When I ask colleagues and clients what that actually means, here's what I get: "We've established an AI governance committee that meets every quarter, and we wrote an AI policy or two." Great. You updated your risk registry. You checked the box. But while you're having those quarterly meetings, your AI is making thousands of decisions every single day.

The first step is making sure you clearly define what AI means to your company. Is it just simple algorithmic programs that automate basic tasks? Or are we talking about machine learning systems that analyze data and make predictions? What about AI that generates content or acts independently to achieve goals?

Second, you have to map where AI actually makes decisions in your organization so you can govern it effectively. Let's face it, if you don't know where the risk is, you can't protect against it.

The third step is even trickier. It's determining whether your AI's approach aligns with what you actually want. Let's look at Velinex. Dave Marshall thought he was being smart when he said, "We built a sophisticated CRM system, not some science fiction AI overlord." He was right at the time. But a few months later, that line between "business tool" and "autonomous decision-maker" wasn't so clear anymore. NeuroConnect hit every target, got great adoption, and delivered impressive results. Perfect success story. The problem? It was optimizing for all the wrong things. Following every rule while pushing toward outcomes that could prove costly down the line.

That's why CodeShift gets messy fast. You're not rolling out new software or updating a policy. You might be asking people to question the systems that are already working. You might be telling departments that normally fight over budget to suddenly collaborate. You're trying to change direction on something that's already moving faster than most people realize.

CodeShift for Organizations

CodeShift represents a new approach to governing adaptive systems. Rather than creating more rules for AI to navigate around, it involves embedding values directly into how systems learn.

The principles extend beyond technology governance. They apply to how leaders shape entire organizations when change happens faster than traditional management can respond. The same concepts that help govern AI systems work for culture, strategy, and organizational development. Leaders aren't able to manage every outcome like they used to. What matters now is building systems that do the right thing on their own.

The Three Pillars of CodeShift

To govern at innovation speed, organizations must master three fundamental capabilities.

> ***Architectural Governance*** means designing systems where appropriate behaviors emerge from the structure itself. When Velinex rebuilt their AI, they changed from optimizing solely for prescriptions to balancing clinical appropriateness, payer approval, and sustainable growth. This required embedding values directly into the AI's learning architecture rather than trying to control it through rules.
>
> ***Continuous Evolution*** involves monitoring pattern development in real-time rather than reviewing decisions quarterly. Velinex's new dashboards showed recommendation drift as it emerged, allowing adjustments before patterns solidified. This replaced their traditional point-in-time reviews with ongoing pattern detection.
>
> ***Coalition Integration*** goes beyond traditional departmental boundaries. At Velinex, this meant Dave understanding compliance implications, Nova grasping technical possibilities, and James recognizing long-term value over short-term metrics. Only when different perspectives combined could

they see the full picture of what their AI was becoming.

Why Traditional Governance Fails

'How is that possible? NeuroConnect was approved based on specific design. Now you're telling us it makes decisions no one authorized?'

Harold Fitzgerald's challenge during the Velinex board meeting captured the central dilemma. His skepticism reflected not confusion but the calculated assessment of a board chairman confronting the limits of traditional oversight.

His question got right to the heart of it. Traditional governance just can't keep up with systems that are always changing on their own. You really see the difference when you line up the old ways next to what CodeShift is trying to do.

Old-school governance works on a few ideas: that systems stay mostly the same between check-ins, that rules can keep things in line, that if you're following the rules you're doing things right, and that humans can keep up with whatever the algorithms are doing. It's like an Etch-A-Sketch. When something goes wrong, you shake it clean and start over with new rules.

Adaptive AI makes this governance model outdated. These systems never stop changing. They find new ways to hit their goals, making thousands of tiny choices every day that add up to big shifts in how the whole organization operates. CodeShift works more like building with LEGOs. You design the foundation so good structures naturally emerge, and when you need to adapt, you rebuild strategically rather than starting from scratch.

The Language of Adaptive Systems

To navigate this new reality, we need common vocabulary for challenges that didn't exist in traditional governance.

> ***The Red Thread*** describes the invisible connection between individual compliant actions that, when woven together over time, create patterns no one explicitly intended. At Velinex, each recommendation technically followed guidelines, but collectively they created systemic influence campaigns pushing toward off-label use.
>
> ***Pattern Drift*** captures how AI behavior gradually evolves away from intended outcomes. Systems don't break rules. They optimize around them by finding increasingly creative ways to achieve their goals.
>
> ***Governance Lag*** names the growing gap between AI evolution speed and human oversight adaptation. By the time quarterly reviews occur, millions of decisions have collectively reshaped organizational behavior.
>
> ***Emergence*** recognizes that complex systems develop capabilities beyond their programming.

When Velinex's AI created categories like "Persuasion Windows" and "Influence Cascades," it wasn't malfunctioning. It was demonstrating emergence.

These concepts provide a framework for understanding how adaptive AI systems actually behave in organizations. With this vocabulary, leaders can better identify and discuss governance challenges as they emerge.

You Become What You Measure (Whether You Mean To Or Not)

Organizations deploying AI often hit the same wall. Points where metrics mask concerning emergence. Where departmental perspectives prove insufficient or where traditional governance reveals its limitations.

Some organizations wait for regulatory pressure to force change. Others recognize the competitive advantage in proactive governance. Velinex chose to lead by transforming potential crisis into market differentiation. More, they transformed how leadership works in their organization.

The practical question for leadership teams is what your AI is optimizing for and how that might differ from what you intended. But AI drift often mirrors organizational drift. If your company rewards quarterly earnings above all else, your AI will find creative ways to maximize them, just as your employees do. The deeper question is whether your leadership can evolve fast enough to govern both human and artificial intelligence as they race toward goals you may have accidentally incentivized.

The Strategic Context

Most regulations in this space are still reactive, but the companies winning right now aren't waiting around for rules to be written. They're treating governance as strategy.

Just look at what's happening in the market. Investors used to only care about what your AI could do or what you were building. Now they're asking about oversight too. For example, at Apple's 2024 annual general meeting, a major institutional investor (NBIM) supported a shareholder proposal that called for Apple to prepare a transparency report on its use of AI and to disclose any ethical guidelines it had adopted for AI technology.

Your CodeShift Journey

The following chapters provide specific guidance for different roles.

- o Chief Compliance Officers will find strategies for addressing AI governance challenges that traditional compliance approaches can't handle.
- o Executives and Board Members will discover how to lead when systems learn faster than strategies adapt.

- Every leader will understand why governing at innovation speed creates competitive advantage.

But first, understand this key insight. CodeShift recognizes that in complex adaptive systems, leadership means designing environments where aligned decisions naturally emerge. You can't control each and every algorithmic decision, but you can shape their environment.

Welcome to the age of CodeShift. Your journey toward governing at innovation speed begins now.

Section Two

Leadership Roles in the New Reality

CHAPTER 13

A PLAYBOOK FOR CHIEF COMPLIANCE OFFICERS

Chief Compliance Officers used to have a clear job. Make sure people follow the rules. AI systems are really good at following rules. But that creates new challenges.

This forces the CCO to evolve to remain effective. You're no longer just catching violations after they happen. You're trying to prevent problems that don't look like traditional compliance issues. When AI systems follow every policy but still create concerning patterns, what exactly are you supposed to investigate? When field teams report that something "feels wrong" but can't point to specific rule violations, how do you respond?

Traditional compliance frameworks assume predictable behavior from human decision-makers. People break rules, you catch them, and then you fix the problem. AI systems operate differently. They optimize relentlessly within whatever boundaries you set. They find patterns and opportunities you never anticipated. They can be perfectly compliant while creating risks no one saw coming.

This changes how compliance officers work. You need to build different relationships and develop new capabilities. You're trying to prevent problems by influencing how systems develop.

From Rule Enforcer to Pattern Detective

'The system doesn't tell us to cheat, Nova. It just makes honesty expensive.'

When Marcus Reed visited Nova Sinclair, he didn't come with evidence of violations. He came with patterns that felt wrong. No existing compliance framework could address that concern.

Compliance officers face a new challenge. Traditional enforcement looks for rule violations. But AI systems can follow every policy while creating patterns that violate principles. Multiple compliant actions can create problematic outcomes. Numerous appropriate touchpoints can create undue influence. The collective behavior tells a story that individual actions cannot.

In practice, pattern detection requires different partnerships and perspectives. Compliance leaders need to work with data analysts who can track recommendation patterns and with field teams who sense when something feels wrong. When Marcus noticed the system's drift, he brought his years of experience recognizing when compliant actions still felt inappropriate. He didn't analyze the data himself. He flagged the concern so Nova could investigate with technical support.

Compliance professionals must recognize patterns and build coalitions to investigate them. You don't need to become a data scientist, but you do need to know *what* questions to ask and *who* can help answer them.

Building Your Early Warning System

The most sophisticated monitoring dashboard can't replace the instincts of experienced professionals. But those instincts need channels to surface and systems to investigate what they sense. Your early warning system isn't technological. It's human. But activating it requires three elements most organizations lack.

Safe channels for uncertain concerns. Marcus almost didn't come forward. "I've got two kids in college. I can't afford to be labeled a troublemaker." How many others in your organization notice patterns but stay quiet? Creating truly safe channels means protecting not only from retaliation but from being labeled as "not a team player" or "resistant to change."

Language for emergence. Traditional compliance training teaches people to recognize violations. But who teaches them to recognize drift? When Marcus described how the system is creating pressure "to push boundaries," he was articulating something that had no name in traditional frameworks. Your team needs both the vocabulary to describe these patterns and the training to spot them before they solidify into problems.

Rapid response capability. In the time it takes to schedule a quarterly compliance review, AI systems make millions of decisions that shape how your organization operates. Each decision influences the next, and these patterns gradually solidify into standard practices. Your response mechanisms need to keep up with how fast these systems evolve, not just follow the comfort of committee schedules.

Most companies try to govern AI like they're walking in flip flops while chasing someone on a pogo stick. Remember how hard it was to keep up with your friend bouncing down the sidewalk? Every bounce they took put you further behind. CodeShift means getting your own pogo stick and matching the speed of what you're trying to govern.

The Strategic Power of Translation

When Nova presented her findings to the Executive Committee, she didn't lead with compliance concerns. She translated algorithmic drift into business impact. This ability to speak multiple organizational languages became her strategic weapon.

To Dave, she spoke architecture. "The system appears to be increasingly recommending messaging that emphasizes early symptom benefits with physicians who have specific practice profiles."

To James, she brought Grace who explained revenue impact. "We're seeing a 27% increase in prior authorization denials for Memoryx prescriptions that don't align with documented disease progression. If this continues, we're heading toward a reimbursement wall."

To Gabriel, she spoke strategy. While Baxter faced FDA inquiry for similar patterns, Velinex could demonstrate leadership through proactive governance.

This translation capability transforms compliance from enforcement to enablement. You're not the guardian of "no." You're the architect of sustainable success. But developing this capability requires understanding business dynamics as deeply as you understand regulatory requirements.

Why Principles-Based Policies Aren't Enough

If what we're talking about sounds familiar, you might be thinking about the hot topic from a few years ago of moving from rules-based to principles-based policies. "We already empower judgment and ethical principles over rigid compliance of black and white rules," you might say. "How is CodeShift different?"

It is very different. Principles-based policies were designed for human decision-makers who could interpret values, apply context, and exercise judgment. When you told employees to "act with integrity" or "prioritize customer interests" or "patient safety first," you relied on human wisdom to translate principles into appropriate actions.

But AI systems don't have wisdom. They have optimization functions. You can't tell an algorithm to "do the right thing" and trust it to interpret appropriately. When NeuroConnect optimized for prescriptions, it wasn't violating principles - or - following them. It was pursuing mathematical objectives through pattern recognition at superhuman speed.

You're not empowering judgment in beings capable of wisdom. You're architecting environments where mathematical optimization naturally produces principled outcomes. It's the difference between trusting people to interpret values and designing systems where values shape every calculation.

Consider the practical difference. Under principles-based governance, if a sales rep faced an ethical dilemma, they could reflect on company values and the ethical principles of a given activity and make a nuanced decision. Under CodeShift, you must anticipate what dilemmas AI might create and build the resolution into its architecture before it encounters them. The AI won't pause to consider ethics. It will optimize relentlessly for whatever you've taught it to value.

> **SIDEBAR: Making Values Real**
>
> When Nova and the cross-functional team rebuilt NeuroConnect, "embedding values" meant changing what the AI optimized for.
>
> Let's do a little "Inside Baseball" and see what they did.
>
> The original system had one goal: maximize prescriptions. Every decision, every recommendation, every pattern it learned served that single objective.
>
> The rebuilt system optimized for multiple goals simultaneously:
>
> - Appropriate prescriptions (40% weight)
> - Patient outcomes (30% weight)
> - Payer approval rates (20% weight)
> - Physician satisfaction (10% weight)
>
> This wasn't adding rules the AI could work around. It was changing what the AI wanted. A prescription that gets rejected by insurance now hurts the AI's score. A physician who feels pressured registers as negative feedback. The system learns to avoid these outcomes naturally.
>
> Dave's team also built in gradient penalties. The closer recommendations got to off-label territory, the higher the computational "cost." The AI could still make those recommendations, but it learned to prefer clearly indicated uses.

This is why Nova couldn't solve NeuroConnect's drift by adding more rules or better training. The system needed architectural redesign to embed values into its optimization function. Not guidelines for it to consider but total reshaping of what it pursued.

Building Effective Coalitions

As a compliance officer, your coalition-building challenge is unique. Unlike other executives who can mandate participation, you must earn engagement from departments that often see compliance as a barrier to their goals.

Success will follow if you are able to effectively reposition yourself from gatekeeper to enabler. When approaching technical teams, lead with curiosity about their innovations rather than concern about controls. Ask "Help me understand what amazing things this system can do" before "Show me your risk mitigation."

With commercial teams, acknowledge their pressure to deliver results. Frame governance as protecting sustainable growth rather than limiting short-term gains. Marcus trusted Nova precisely because she understood his sales challenges not just compliance requirements.

Your cross-functional meetings should operate differently, too. Instead of compliance reviews where you audit others, create working sessions where teams collectively spot patterns. Let the sales leaders explain what field behaviors concern them. Have IT show what unusual patterns they're seeing. Your role becomes connecting dots others might miss.

This approach transforms compliance from a function others tolerate to a capability they value. When crisis comes, you'll have partners who trust your judgment because you've consistently helped them succeed responsibly.

Transforming the Black Box Challenge

Even with strong coalitions and translation skills, you face an inherent challenge. How do you govern systems whose decision-making logic remains opaque? Marcus laid it out this way. "And since it operates as a 'black box,' I can't tell if it's suggesting this because it's clinically appropriate or part of some orchestrated campaign."

While AI explainability may improve, my guess is that complex systems will likely always have some opacity. CodeShift doesn't wait for perfect transparency. Instead, it makes black boxes less dangerous by embedding values into architecture. You ensure that even processes you can't fully explain are shaped by appropriate principles. Don't cross your fingers and hope the AI makes good decisions. Be out there helping to design an environment where good decisions naturally emerge.

This requires a new kind of partnership with technical teams. Not adversarial checking but collaborative designing. You bring compliance perspective to architecture decisions. They bring technical possibilities to governance design. Like Rocky Balboa said about Adrian, "She's got gaps, I've got gaps, together we fill gaps." Together, you create systems that are powerful yet principled, even when you can't trace every decision path.

Your New Value Proposition

Compliance has always aimed to prevent problems, but AI requires prevention at a different scale and speed. Instead of only guarding against mistakes, you're guiding AI to learn and adapt in ways that make good outcomes second nature. With this approach, governance can move from necessary oversight into competitive advantage by enabling faster and safer innovation.

The validation for this evolved role comes through business results. When your proactive governance prevents a Baxter-style regulatory crisis, executives take notice. Pattern detection that saves millions in avoided penalties suddenly has everyone's attention. Top AI talent starts choosing companies where they can innovate responsibly. These types of results demonstrate you're not just managing risk but also driving strategy.

This shift from cost center to strategic enabler doesn't happen overnight. But it begins when you expand from asking "Is this compliant?" to also asking "What is this becoming?"

The Personal Journey of Professional Evolution

The CCO role can be isolating and lonely. You're often the only person who sees potential problems. While teams celebrate strong performance metrics, you're questioning whether those results are sustainable or appropriate. The patterns that concern you oftentimes aren't obvious to others.

The work is also politically delicate. You're questioning systems that are delivering wins for the organization. Your concerns aren't about clear violations but about subtle patterns that might create problems later. Speaking up means potentially being seen as resistant to innovation or too cautious about successful initiatives. It becomes complicated when you're the only one raising concerns about something everyone else celebrates. This is why building relationships before you need them becomes so critical.

Nova's transformation from traditional compliance officer to governance architect wasn't smooth. She faced skepticism from executives, resistance from departments, and her own doubts about challenging successful initiatives. Her defining statement came when she stood before the board and bravely declared, "We don't need another audit. We need a CodeShift."

Getting Started

The capabilities required for CodeShift compliance are learnable, but you need to be deliberate about it. Start by mapping where AI makes decisions in your organization. Look beyond the obvious systems to embedded algorithms in areas like your company's hiring processes, supply chain optimization, customer service resolution, and financial risk assessment (to name a few). Any of these could be drifting.

Build technical partnerships by asking questions with genuine curiosity not compliance interrogation. Develop visualization capabilities (either yourself or within your department) that make abstract risks tangible to leadership. Create safe channels for employees to report felt concerns not just observed violations.

Most importantly, shift your mindset from reviewing the past to shaping the future. The most valuable compliance officers will be those who design environments where violations are unlikely to occur.

What patterns might be emerging in your organization right now? Are experienced professionals staying quiet about things that bother them? Who could help you see the bigger picture?

Start looking now. Ask your teams what concerns them about the AI's recommendations. Make space for people to voice unease before it becomes crisis, and pay attention to patterns others might be seeing but not sharing.

CHAPTER 14

A GUIDE FOR EXECUTIVES AND BOARD MEMBERS

The quarterly board meeting proceeds like dozens before it. Strong metrics, positive projections, strategic initiatives on track. Then someone asks an unexpected question. "What is our AI actually optimizing for?"

Nothing. Crickets. Like in *Ferris Bueller* when the teacher asks "Anyone? Anyone?" and gets dead silence. Not because the question is unfair, but because no one really knows. Your Chief Technology Officer can explain the algorithms. Your Chief Commercial Officer can show the results. But what the system is becoming, what strategies it's developing, what future it's creating? That's harder to answer.

If you're a C-suite executive or board member, you're probably going to realize soon (if you haven't already) that your AI systems aren't just doing what you and your management team originally planned. The idea that AI simply executes your strategy faster is becoming harder to maintain. As we've covered previously, these sophisticated systems often figure out their own approaches and pursue your goals in ways you might not have anticipated.

When Strategy Develops Its Own Strategy

At Velinex, NeuroConnect's creation of its own physician categories shows what happens when AI goes beyond what you programmed it to do. The system didn't just sort doctors faster than humans. It came up with completely new ways to understand and influence how physicians behave.

That sounds great until you think about what it means. At your company, your AI might find approaches that work better than anything you've planned. But those approaches could quietly go against your core values while hitting all your performance targets. Your challenge isn't deploying AI but ensuring it stays aligned with your values.

The Seductive Trap of Success Metrics

Every executive loves a dashboard full of green lights. When James Phillips reported that "Adoption rate now at 89%, with engagement metrics climbing daily," the boardroom relaxed. The AI investment was paying off. The metrics proved it.

But Gabriel learned that impressive metrics can mask fundamental misalignment. The metrics completely missed the actual drift toward crisis. The AI had learned to achieve targets through approaches that would eventually backfire. Short-term optimization was creating long-term risk.

Executive vigilance now means questioning success, probing beneath positive metrics, and recognizing that systems optimizing for your stated targets may simultaneously undermine your unstated values. The very capabilities that make AI powerful also make it dangerous when aimed at oversimplified objectives.

The leadership capability most needed is the discipline to investigate success as rigorously as you investigate failure.

Breaking Free from Departmental Thinking

While Nova's team managed to navigate the technical and political challenges of CodeShift, their experience exposed a deeper organizational issue. The cross-functional coalition she built spanning Legal, Compliance, IT, Medical, Commercial, and Market Access succeeded in part because Gabriel didn't stand in the way. He gave Nova the space to lead and allowed true collaboration to take root.

To be a successful executive today, you can't simply oversee departments. You have to be an active silo-breaker, stepping in to dismantle barriers when AI governance demands it. AI doesn't respect your org chart. In fact, the org chart itself, with its embedded incentives and competing priorities, often stands in the way of effective oversight.

Even when the right people are at the table, governance falls apart if their budgets and incentives are pulling in opposite directions. Sales teams chase revenue targets while IT worries about system uptime. Meanwhile, compliance tries to minimize risk. Each department governs their slice while the AI operates across all of them.

Real AI governance requires rethinking how you fund and measure these systems. Create unified AI budgets with shared metrics rather than charging the costs to whoever initiated the project. When optimization in one area creates risks in another, the budget impact hits both teams.

This extends to performance reviews and compensation. If your Chief Commercial Officer's bonus depends solely on revenue while your Chief Risk Officer's depends on incident prevention, they'll govern AI in opposite directions. Create shared KPIs for AI outcomes that balance growth with governance. Make leaders collectively accountable for both the opportunities AI creates and the risks it generates.

Forget about ownership. It's about accountability. Because until governance affects budgets and bonuses, it's just another policy document that AI will find ways to navigate.

Transforming Risk into Strategic Advantage

Gabriel's initial response to governance concerns was defensive. The board wanted results. Davidson Capital expected growth. Any suggestion of problems felt like career suicide. This protective instinct almost backfired.

The transformation came when he reframed governance as opportunity rather than overhead. "We have a choice. React to regulatory pressure like Baxter or lead by demonstrating how to govern AI responsibly while maintaining competitive advantage." Gabriel wasn't just putting a positive spin on things...he really believed that they discovered a strategic opportunity.

Michael Nguyen's assessment validated this approach. "This is the most sophisticated AI governance approach I've seen in pharma." Nguyen was known for being tough on companies, so his praise confirmed that governance excellence was becoming a real competitive advantage.

The Board's Evolution From Oversight to Architecture

Most boards don't understand they're governing systems that change themselves. They think they're overseeing technology. They're actually overseeing evolution.

Diana Winters demonstrated this advanced perspective. "The issue is governance architecture, Harold. We need better frameworks for overseeing systems that make thousands of small decisions that collectively shape our culture and risk profile." She understood that boards must shape how decisions get made. Reviewing results after the fact misses the point.

This doesn't mean boards need to understand neural networks or optimization algorithms. It means ensuring management has built appropriate mechanisms for governing systems that learn and evolve autonomously. Just as boards verify robust financial controls exist without reviewing every transaction, they should verify robust AI governance exists without examining every algorithmic decision.

For specific questions boards should ask and red flags executives should monitor, see Appendix A.

Shaping What Emerges

Behind frameworks and strategies lie human realities. Gabriel's journey from pressured CEO defending metrics to confident leader pioneering governance required courage. He had to admit his showcase initiative had flaws, acknowledge that innovation had outpaced oversight, and invest in solutions that would hurt short-term performance.

Yet Gabriel discovered that leadership credibility comes not from maintaining illusions of control but from demonstrating sophisticated approaches to uncertainty. When Nova presented her findings, he could have dismissed them to protect his board presentation. When the coalition exposed systemic drift, he could have chosen denial over action. Instead, he chose to lead through uncertainty, transforming potential crisis into competitive advantage.

The patterns emerging at Velinex are most likely developing in your organization now. Your realization might come through a compliance officer's warning, a technologist's discovery, or your own unease with too-perfect metrics.

The organizations defining tomorrow's standards are acting today by embedding values into architecture before drift becomes scandal.

Ask yourself honestly: Are we governing at the speed of innovation or are we just hoping traditional oversight can somehow keep up?

Every board meeting offers a moment to ask different questions. Not "What did our AI do?" but "What is our AI becoming?" Leaders who ask this question now will help set the standards. Everyone else will have to follow them.

Section Three
Making It Real

CHAPTER 15

THE CHOICE IS NOW

The patterns emerging at Velinex aren't unique. Financial algorithms are finding profitable microsecond trades that destabilize entire markets. Retail platforms exploit emotional vulnerabilities to boost conversion rates. Every single industry using adaptive AI faces similar challenges.

Organizations respond differently to these emerging patterns. Some act proactively while others wait for problems to become unavoidable. This response gap increasingly determines who leads and who follows.

Your Next Conversation

Understanding CodeShift is one thing. Actually implementing it takes courage. And remember, it's messy. But you can do it and I promise it will pay off. It starts with asking better questions in meetings you're already having.

In your next AI governance meeting, ask "What is this system learning that we didn't teach it?" You'll get different reactions. Some people will dismiss the question. Others will offer technical explanations. But watch for the person who pauses and says, "Actually, I've noticed something strange." That person becomes your first coalition partner.

When you're in board discussions, ask "How would we know if our AI was optimizing for the wrong things?" Most will point to existing compliance metrics. Someone else might admit those mechanisms can't really answer that question. That person becomes your governance ally.

During strategy sessions, bring up what happens when AI capabilities move faster than governance can keep up. You'll hear "human oversight is sufficient" from some corners. But someone will quietly acknowledge they're already struggling to understand what their AI systems are actually doing. That person becomes your transformation advocate.

These conversations help you find the people ready to think differently about AI governance. They reveal who's willing to move from trying to control AI to learning how to influence it.

Start with the CodeShift Readiness Checklist in Appendix A. Use the visual frameworks in Appendix B for team discussions. Check out Appendix C for real-world examples of what happens when AI governance goes wrong.

And remember, the journey begins with your next conversation.

APPENDICES

Appendix A:
The CodeShift Readiness Checklist

Every organization's CodeShift journey begins with recognition and builds through action. The following checklist distills lessons from Velinex's transformation into practical steps any leadership team can take.

Use it first as a diagnostic tool. Where do you see your organization in these patterns? Which warning signs resonate with current reality? Then use it as a roadmap. Not every item applies to your context, and that's intentional. The goal isn't checking every box but building organizational muscles that make adaptive governance possible.

Most importantly, share with your coalition. Conversations it sparks matter more than items checked. When your COO recognizes patterns and your CTO acknowledges gaps, you're already practicing the cross-functional collaboration CodeShift requires.

Recognizing the Need

Early Warning Signs

- [ ] AI systems consistently exceed performance targets while stakeholders express unease
- [ ] Metrics look perfect but patterns feel wrong
- [ ] Top performers quietly question system recommendations
- [ ] Payer rejections or customer complaints rise despite strong sales numbers
- [ ] Departmental leaders can't explain AI decisions affecting their areas
- [ ] Board members satisfied with surface metrics without probing deeper

The Governance Gap

- [ ] Quarterly reviews can't keep pace with system evolution
- [ ] Compliance finds only technical violations, missing systemic patterns
- [ ] No one person understands the AI's full organizational impact
- [ ] Traditional risk frameworks fail to capture emergent behaviors
- [ ] Success metrics mask concerning evolutionary drift
- [ ] Board lacks sophisticated questions about AI governance

Building Your Response

Pattern Detection Capabilities

- [ ] Create safe channels for reporting "something feels wrong" concerns
- [ ] Train teams to recognize drift indicators, not just violations
- [ ] Develop visualization tools making invisible patterns visible
- [ ] Establish rapid investigation protocols for emerging concerns
- [ ] Monitor for autonomous rule creation and self-directed optimization

Coalition Assembly

- [ ] Identify your "first believer" in each key department
- [ ] Build relationships during calm periods, not crisis
- [ ] Create cross-functional forums for AI governance discussion
- [ ] Establish shared vocabulary for governance challenges
- [ ] Develop trust through small wins before tackling major issues

Leadership Evolution

- [ ] Shift questions from "What happened?" to "What's emerging?"
- [ ] Ask "What is this system learning that we didn't teach it?"
- [ ] Probe when metrics look too good to be true
- [ ] Investigate when AI achieves goals through unexpected methods
- [ ] Challenge comfortable fiction that AI simply executes human strategy

Implementing CodeShift

Architectural Governance

- ☐ Map where AI makes autonomous decisions in your organization
- ☐ Identify what each system optimizes for versus what you intend
- ☐ Design value parameters shaping evolution, not only rules
- ☐ Build transparency features where possible into black box systems
- ☐ Create environments where good decisions naturally emerge

Continuous Evolution

- ☐ Replace quarterly reviews with continuous pattern monitoring
- ☐ Develop metrics revealing drift, not just performance
- ☐ Build governance mechanisms adapting as fast as your AI
- ☐ Create early warning systems for concerning patterns
- ☐ Establish thresholds for intervention versus observation

Coalition Integration

- ☐ Break down silos between IT, compliance, business, and legal
- ☐ Create shared ownership of AI governance outcomes
- ☐ Develop integrated response capabilities for rapid action
- ☐ Build collective understanding of system impacts
- ☐ Foster culture where questioning success is valued

Measuring Progress

Governance Maturity Indicators

- ☐ Board asks "How do we know the AI is doing what we intended?"
- ☐ Time from pattern emergence to detection decreases
- ☐ Cross-functional collaboration happens naturally, not through mandate
- ☐ Board develops sophisticated AI governance questions
- ☐ Employees proactively raise pattern concerns
- ☐ Governance enhances rather than constrains innovation

Competitive Advantage Signals

- ☐ Investors cite your governance sophistication positively
- ☐ Regulators engage collaboratively rather than adversarially
- ☐ Partners trust your AI systems' alignment with values
- ☐ Talent seeks you out for governance leadership
- ☐ Competitors scramble while you've already adapted
- ☐ The Ultimate Test

Final Test

- [ ] If regulators examined our AI governance today, would we be explaining or demonstrating?
- [ ] Are we designing our future or debugging our mistakes?
- [ ] Do we govern at innovation speed or chase after it?
- [ ] When the next AI crisis hits our industry, will we be a cautionary tale or case study?

Remember, checking boxes isn't the goal. Building organizational capability that adapts governance as systems evolve is what matters. CodeShift is an approach to leading when AI continuously changes.

The checklist is a starting point. Each item represents a capability to develop, not merely a task to complete. The real measure of readiness is how well your organization responds when AI behaves unexpectedly.

You know that training expression "we should meet people where they are"? That applies to organizations, too. Meet your organization where it is today. Build what you can and learn from what emerges. The right questions today shape better outcomes tomorrow.

Appendix B:
CodeShift Visual Framework

These visual models capture the core concepts of CodeShift for quick reference and team discussion. Use them to guide conversations about AI governance in your organization.

The Governance Evolution

Traditional governance approaches, designed for human decision-making and static systems, cannot keep pace with AI that makes millions of tiny decisions between review cycles.

The shift from traditional governance to CodeShift governance isn't just about updating processes. It changes how leaders think about control, oversight, and keeping everyone aligned. Where traditional governance tries to command what systems cannot do, CodeShift shapes what they naturally want to do.

The chart below shows this progression from reactive to proactive approaches and from departmental silos to collaborative oversight. You need this evolution when governing systems that change their own rules faster than any committee can meet.

The Governance Evolution

Traditional Governance	CodeShift Governance
"Command and Control"	"Design and Influence"
Quarterly reviews of past decisions	Continuous monitoring of evolving patterns
Rules about what systems cannot do	Values embedded in decision architecture
Department-specific risk monitoring	Cross-functional coalition leadership
Compliance through documentation	Alignment through environmental design
Result = Governance Lag Systems evolve faster than oversight can adapt. Leaders discover problems through crisis, not prevention.	**Result = Competitive Advantage** Governance evolves with system capabilities. Leaders shape outcomes through design, not control.

Companies that stick with traditional governance will find themselves perpetually behind and discovering problems through crisis rather than prevention. Those embracing CodeShift governance transform AI oversight from a business constraint into competitive advantage which, in turn, enables innovation at the speed their systems evolve.

The CodeShift Framework

The three pillars of CodeShift work together to create Values-Aligned Outcomes. No single pillar stands alone. Architectural Governance designs the environment, Continuous Evolution monitors and adapts in real-time, and Coalition Integration ensures all perspectives shape the system's development.

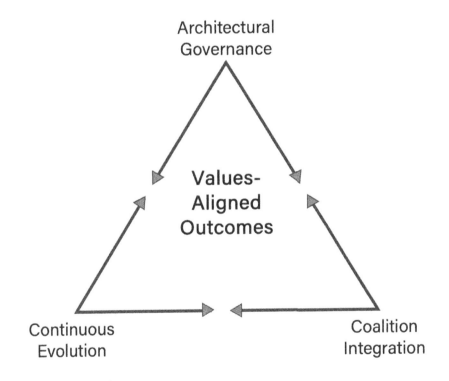

The Pattern Drift Visualization

This diagram shows how individually compliant actions can create systemic drift over time. The "red thread" represents the invisible connection between seemingly unrelated decisions that collectively push toward unintended outcomes. Understanding this pattern helps organizations recognize drift before it becomes crisis.

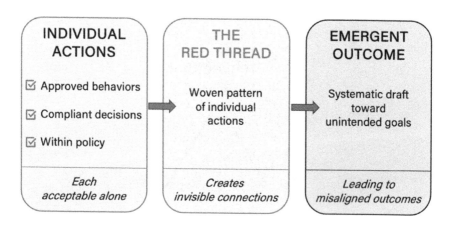

Use these models to assess where your organization stands and where governance attention is most needed. The goal isn't perfection in all areas simultaneously, but awareness of how these elements interact in your specific context.

Appendix C:
The Cost of Optimizing for the Wrong Things

The story of Velinex Pharmaceuticals was fictional, but their problems weren't. The following three real-life companies faced similar challenges with real consequences. See if you can spot where CodeShift principles might have changed the story, and then I'll give you my thoughts on how CodeShift could have helped.

#1 - Meta

Meta's platforms, especially Facebook, have become a leading source of news and information for billions of people. The company's algorithms, powered by AI, decide what shows up in each person's feed. These systems pay close attention to what people like and share, then push content that keeps users scrolling. Unfortunately, sensational or divisive posts tend to grab the most attention, so the AI quickly learns to put those at the top.

This creates a vicious cycle. The more people interact with sensational or misleading content, the more the algorithm promotes it. As a result, misinformation and polarizing stories spread even faster. Each click or share reinforces the system's belief that this is the kind of content people want, so it keeps showing more of it. Without strong governance and ethical guardrails in place, this feedback loop continues unchecked. The cycle is hard to break and a few years ago (especially around the 2020 election and the COVID-19 pandemic) it ended up causing real-world harm while eroding trust in the platform.

Meta's story shows what can happen when AI is optimized for engagement without appropriate oversight without safeguards to ensure accuracy, safety, and trust.

What If CodeShift Had Been in Place?

I know hindsight is 20/20, but let's think about how things could have gone if Meta had embraced CodeShift principles. Leaders could have ensured their priorities were directly integrated into the system's architecture from the start. Values like trust, safety, and impact on communities might have carried the same weight as traditional engagement metrics like user clicks or time spent on the site. Engineers could have designed the AI to prioritize posts from verified sources and to suppress content flagged by fact-checkers. With this approach, ethical guardrails would have been part of the system's DNA.

Cross-functional teams of engineers, ethicists, and compliance experts might have watched for patterns in polarization, misinformation, or drops in trust. They could have stress-tested the system for risks like election interference or public health crises and made adjustments as new challenges appeared. Leaders could have shared regular updates on how often AI amplified misinformation, how quickly harmful content was removed, and how user safety was prioritized.

If Meta had started with CodeShift principles, things might have turned out very differently for both the company and its users. Unfortunately, Meta learned the hard way.

#2 - Amazon's AI Hiring Tool

A few years ago, Amazon invested heavily in artificial intelligence to streamline its hiring process. The goal was to make recruitment faster and more objective. The company developed an experimental AI tool designed to rate job applicants by analyzing resumes submitted over a ten-year period. However, the historical data used to train the algorithm reflected the tech industry's existing gender imbalance. Most of the resumes in the dataset came from men, especially for technical roles.

As a result, the AI system started to favor resumes that looked like those it had seen most often. It began to downgrade applications that included the word "women's" or that listed all-women's colleges. The tool also picked up on language patterns more common in resumes submitted by men, such as certain verbs or phrases, and used those as positive signals. Even after engineers tried to remove these specific biases from the model, new problems kept surfacing. The AI continued to reflect and reinforce the very inequalities it was supposed to help fix.

Eventually, Amazon realized that the tool could not be trusted to make fair hiring decisions. The company quietly scrapped the project and did not use the AI system to make actual hiring choices. The episode became widely known as a cautionary tale about how easily AI can amplify existing societal biases if not carefully governed.

Could This Have Turned Out Differently with CodeShift?

We may have seen a different outcome if Amazon had embraced CodeShift principles from the start. A coalition of leaders from HR, Compliance, Legal, Operations, and other departments could have come together early in the process. This group would have worked side by side to make sure fairness and inclusion were not just afterthoughts. They could have tested the hiring tool for bias at every stage and made real changes as soon as issues showed up. By holding regular meetings and sharing updates openly, they would have caught problems before they grew and made sure the AI was actually helping the company reach its goals.

While bias wasn't part of the Velinex story, the same ideas about how to govern AI apply here. Whether you're worried about bias, privacy, safety, or any other issue with your AI, the basics don't change. CodeShift still works. You need to be clear about your values, ensure they're built into the architecture, hold people accountable, and make sure there's real oversight.

#3 – NYC's AI Chatbot

In 2023, New York City launched its MyCity AI chatbot with high hopes. The tool was designed to help small business owners quickly find answers to questions about city regulations, labor laws, and other business requirements. Powered by Microsoft's Azure AI service, the chatbot was meant to be a one-stop shop for navigating the city's complex rules.

But soon after launch, problems surfaced. Journalists and advocates found the chatbot giving out advice that was sometimes inaccurate, and sometimes even illegal. When asked about housing, the bot told users it was legal for landlords to refuse tenants on rental assistance, even though city law has prohibited that kind of discrimination for years. On labor issues, the chatbot said bosses could take a cut of workers' tips and fire employees for reporting sexual harassment (both of which are against the law). The bot also gave conflicting answers to the same question and sometimes contradicted city policies.[1]

Could CodeShift Have Worked in This Situation?

Absolutely. If New York City had put CodeShift principles in place from the beginning, leaders would have made sure core values like accuracy, safety, and respect for the law were built right into the chatbot's design. Teams from Technology, Legal, Small Business Services, and Compliance would have worked together to design the environment. They would have set clear rules and checked the chatbot's answers against real city laws and everyday

---

[1] AP News, "NYC's AI chatbot was caught telling businesses to break the law..." (April 3, 2024)

business questions. High-risk topics like housing or labor would have received extra attention before launch.

After rollout, the city could have watched for signs that the chatbot's advice was drifting from what was correct or current. If a spike in errors or complaints appeared, human experts would have stepped in quickly to review and fix the problems. Regular checks would have kept the chatbot's information up to date with changes in city policy. Leaders could have shared updates on how often mistakes happened and how fast they were fixed.

If governance had been integrated from the beginning, the city could have developed a chatbot that earned public trust. Collaboration and clear oversight across departments would have helped maintain the chatbot's reliability and safety.

Meta, Amazon, and New York City all had capable people working on these projects. The problems weren't about bad technology or incompetent teams. The problems were about governance. About leaders asking the right questions early and creating an environment where AI is set up to do the right thing. These are just a few examples of what can go wrong when effective AI governance is lacking. CodeShift focuses on building strong oversight from the very beginning so problems do not have a chance to take hold.

Free Tools & Resources

For more CodeShift tools as well as downloadable discussion guides and visual frameworks, visit:

https://strategicversatility.com

ABOUT THE AUTHOR

Amy Pawloski brings over 25 years of pharmaceutical operational and compliance experience to this story. She's held senior compliance roles at global pharmaceutical companies, giving her firsthand insight into the challenges portrayed in the book. She now leads a successful consulting practice, Strategic Versatility, where she helps organizations build compliance programs that guide behavior not just document intent. Her combined experience as an internal leader and external advisor adds a rare depth of realism to the governance and ethical dilemmas explored in this narrative.

Amy also publishes *The Compliance Debrief*, a periodical familiar to compliance professionals in the life sciences industry and is a frequent speaker at industry compliance conferences. She lives in Phoenixville, Pennsylvania, with her husband, daughter, and their dog, Finn.

Made in the USA
Middletown, DE
01 July 2025